P · O · C · K · E · T · S

WORLD ATLAS

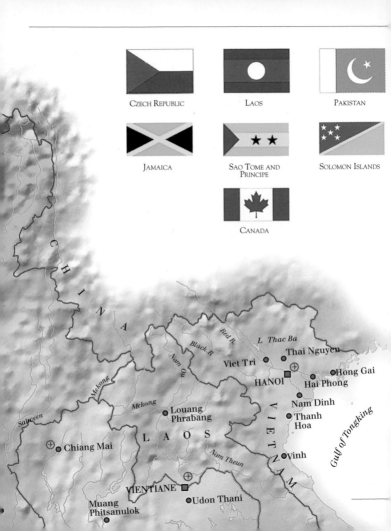

CZECH REPUBLIC

LAOS

PAKISTAN

JAMAICA

SAO TOME AND PRINCIPE

SOLOMON ISLANDS

CANADA

CHINA

Salween

Mekong

Nam Ou

Black R.

Red R.

L. Thac Ba

Thai Nguyen

Viet Tri

HANOI

Hai Phong

Hong Gai

Nam Dinh

Thanh Hoa

Mekong

Louang Phrabang

LAOS

Nam Theun

Vinh

VIETNAM

Gulf of Tongking

Chiang Mai

VIENTIANE

Udon Thani

Muang Phitsanulok

P · O · C · K · E · T · S

WORLD ATLAS

Written by
ESTHER LABI

DORLING KINDERSLEY
London • New York • Moscow • Sydney
www.dk.com

A DORLING KINDERSLEY BOOK
www.dk.com

Editor	Esther Labi
Designer	Carlton Hibbert
Senior editor	Hazel Egerton
Senior art editor	Jacquie Gulliver
Editorial consultant	Joan Dear
Picture research	Lorna Ainger
Production	Ruth Cobb

First published in Great Britain in 1995
by Dorling Kindersley Limited
9 Henrietta Street, London WC2E 8PS

2 4 6 8 10 9 7 5 3 1

Copyright © 1995 Dorling Kindersley Ltd., London
Revised edition 1997

A CIP catalogue record for this book is available from
the British Library

ISBN 0 7513 3028 0

Colour reproduction by Colourscan, Singapore
Printed and bound in Italy by L.E.G.O.

CONTENTS

HOW TO USE THIS BOOK

THESE PAGES SHOW YOU how to use *Pockets: World Atlas*. The maps are organized by continent: North America, Central and South America, Europe, Africa, North and West Asia, South and East Asia, and Australasia. There is also an introductory section at the front and a comprehensive index at the back.

KEY TO ICONS
All the icons used in the Atlas are listed below.

♫ THE ARTS

☁ CLIMATE

🚊 COMMUNICATIONS

☒ ENVIRONMENT

🦋 FLORA AND FAUNA

🏛 HISTORY

🏭 INDUSTRY

⛰ NATURAL FEATURES

👥 PEOPLE

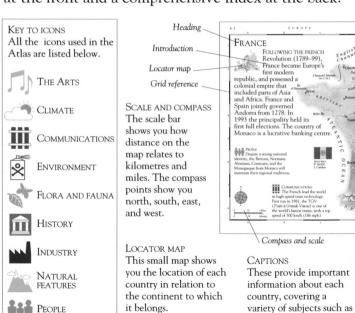

Heading
Introduction
Locator map
Grid reference

SCALE AND COMPASS
The scale bar shows you how distance on the map relates to kilometres and miles. The compass points show you north, south, east, and west.

FRANCE

FOLLOWING THE FRENCH Revolution (1789–99), France became Europe's first modern republic, and possessed a colonial empire that included parts of Asia and Africa. France and Spain jointly governed Andorra from 1278. In 1993 the principality held its first full elections. The country of Monaco is a lucrative banking centre.

👥 PEOPLE
Despite a strong national identity, the Bretons, Normans, Alsatians, Corsicans, and the Monegasque from Monaco still maintain their regional traditions.

🚊 COMMUNICATIONS
The French lead the world in high-speed train technology. First run in 1981, the TGV (*Train à Grande Vitesse*) is one of the world's fastest trains, with a top speed of 300 km/h (186 mph).

Compass and scale

LOCATOR MAP
This small map shows you the location of each country in relation to the continent to which it belongs.

CAPTIONS
These provide important information about each country, covering a variety of subjects such as the environment, people, climate, and history.

INTRODUCTION
This provides you with an overview of the area or region and gives interesting facts about the country's climate, landscape, and political situation.

RUNNING HEADS
These remind you which section you are in. At the top of the left-hand page is the name of the continent. The right-hand page gives the country. This page on France is in the section on Europe.

KEY TO MAPS

INTERNATIONAL BORDER	
DISPUTED BORDER	
STATE BORDER	
CAPITAL CITY	SHINGT D.C.
STATE OR ADMINISTRATIVE CAPITAL	LANTA
MAJOR TOWN	arlesto
AIRPORT	
SEAPORT	
RIVER	
CANAL	
WADI	
LAKE	
SEASONAL LAKE	

Running head

Caption icon

Caption

FLAGS
The flag of each nation is positioned next to the country. Also included are population figures (**P**) and information about the official languages spoken in that area (**L**).

Flag

GRID REFERENCE
The letters and numbers around this grid help you to locate places listed in the index. See page 136 for an explanation on how to use this grid.

GAZETTEER INDEX
A gazetteer index at the back of the book lists all the major towns, cities, rivers, mountain ranges, and lakes that appear in the book.

GUIDE TO MAP PAGES

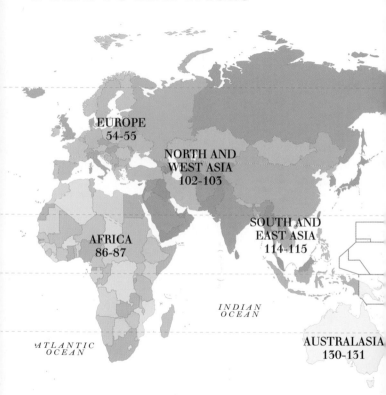

EUROPE
54-55

NORTH AND
WEST ASIA
102-103

SOUTH AND
EAST ASIA
114-115

AFRICA
86-87

*INDIAN
OCEAN*

*ATLANTIC
OCEAN*

AUSTRALASIA
130-131

*SOUTHERN
OCEAN*

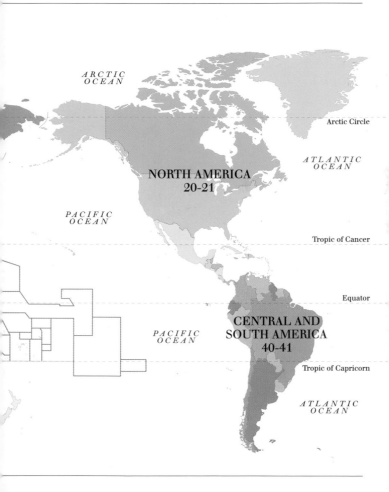

ARCTIC
OCEAN

Arctic Circle

ATLANTIC
OCEAN

NORTH AMERICA
20-21

PACIFIC
OCEAN

Tropic of Cancer

Equator

**CENTRAL AND
SOUTH AMERICA**
40-41

PACIFIC
OCEAN

Tropic of Capricorn

ATLANTIC
OCEAN

THE PLANET EARTH

EARTH, ONE OF nine planets that travel around the Sun, is part of the solar system within a galaxy called the Milky Way. The only planet within our solar system that supports life, Earth has sufficient light, heat, and water to support a wide range of plants and animals. The atmosphere protects the planet by filtering the Sun's rays.

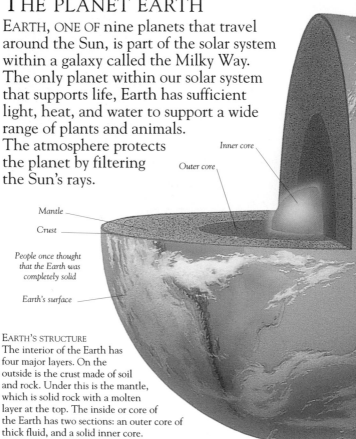

Inner core

Outer core

Mantle

Crust

People once thought that the Earth was completely solid

Earth's surface

EARTH'S STRUCTURE
The interior of the Earth has four major layers. On the outside is the crust made of soil and rock. Under this is the mantle, which is solid rock with a molten layer at the top. The inside or core of the Earth has two sections: an outer core of thick fluid, and a solid inner core.

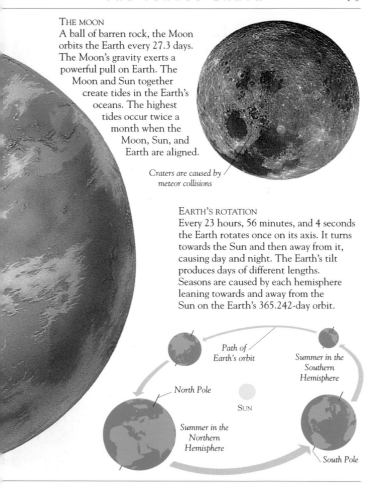

THE MOON
A ball of barren rock, the Moon orbits the Earth every 27.3 days. The Moon's gravity exerts a powerful pull on Earth. The Moon and Sun together create tides in the Earth's oceans. The highest tides occur twice a month when the Moon, Sun, and Earth are aligned.

Craters are caused by meteor collisions

EARTH'S ROTATION
Every 23 hours, 56 minutes, and 4 seconds the Earth rotates once on its axis. It turns towards the Sun and then away from it, causing day and night. The Earth's tilt produces days of different lengths. Seasons are caused by each hemisphere leaning towards and away from the Sun on the Earth's 365.242-day orbit.

Path of Earth's orbit

Summer in the Southern Hemisphere

North Pole

SUN

Summer in the Northern Hemisphere

South Pole

THE MOVING CRUST

THE EARTH'S CRUST is broken up into 15 plates in which the continents are embedded. Some countries lie in the middle of a plate, while others have a plate boundary through them. Forces in the Earth's mantle move the plates slowly around the globe, a process called continental drift. Rift valleys, ocean trenches, and mountains have all formed in areas where plates meet.

The plates of the Earth's crust fit together like a jigsaw puzzle

Hot rocky material circulates under the plates

PLATE MOVEMENT
Plates collide, overlap, and slide past each other as they move around the globe. When plates collide, one plate may be forced under another into the mantle to form a deep ocean trench, or it may push rock upwards to form mountains.

220 MILLION YEARS AGO
Scientists believe that about 220 million years ago the world's continents were part of one giant continent called Pangaea. Over the following 20 million years, it split into Laurasia and Gondwanaland.

100 MILLION YEARS AGO
Africa and South America separated 100 million years ago, breaking away from Antarctica. The Atlantic Ocean was created by a spreading ridge between North America, Europe, and Africa.

PRESENT DAY
Scientists can only guess what the world was like before Pangaea, but if the movement of plates continues, the Great Rift Valley will become an island and Africa and Europe will fuse.

SLIDING PLATES
The San Andreas fault, where two plates are sliding past each other, extends for 965 km (600 miles) in California, U.S.A. Movement between the plates is not steady and pressure builds up, causing earthquakes. About 90 per cent of earthquakes occur in the "Ring of Fire", around the Pacific plate.

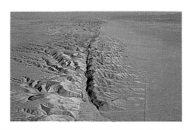

CLIMATE AND VEGETATION

THE MAIN INFLUENCES on an area's climate are its distance from a large body of water, its height above sea level, and the amount of sunlight it receives. Rainfall and sunlight levels are highest at the equator, where the habitats with the most plant and animal life are found: rainforests, mangrove swamps, and coral reefs.

POLAR

Polar regions are so cold that few plants can survive. The treeless tundra regions of Siberia, Canada, Scandinavia, and Alaska support moss and lichens, as well as small flowers and shrubs during summer.

COOL

Coastal areas have less extreme climates than inland regions. Coniferous forests grow in cold northern Asia and North America. Warmer areas have forests of deciduous trees, which lose their leaves in winter.

WARM

Hot, dry summers and wet winters are typical of the Mediterranean region as well as parts of Southern Africa, the Americas, and Australia. Vegetation varies from treeless grasslands to open forests of trees and shrubs.

The world's largest remaining rainforest is in the Amazon Basin, Brazil

DESERT AND DRY LANDS
Arid and semi-arid lands cover more than 30 per cent of the Earth's land surface. Semi-arid regions scattered with grasses and scrubs are called savannah. Cold deserts, like the ice deserts of the Arctic and Antarctic, have no more rain than the Sahara.

TROPICAL
High temperatures and high rainfall are typical of the Tropics. The main difference between tropical and monsoon climates is the distribution of rainfall. Tropical rainforests near the equator depend on year-round rainfall.

The coniferous forests of Asia and northernmost Europe are called taiga

MOUNTAIN
Vegetation on the lower slopes depends on the climate zone in which the mountain is located. Mountains become colder with altitude and only hardy alpine plants grow above the treeline. Snow and bare rock occur above the snowline.

TROPICAL MONSOON
Tropical regions with distinct wet and dry seasons have a monsoon climate. Each year, the monsoon winds reverse their direction completely, forming the two seasons.

Gum trees, or Eucalyptus, have adapted to dry conditions

WORLD TIME ZONES

IMAGINARY LINES are drawn around the globe, either
parallel to the equator (latitude) or from pole to pole
(longitude, or meridians). The Earth is divided into 24
time zones, one for each hour of the day. Greenwich is
on 0° meridian and
time advances by
one hour for every
15° of longitude
east of Greenwich.

TIME ZONES
The numbers on the map
indicate the number of hours
which must be subtracted or
added to reach GMT. When it
is noon at Greenwich, for
example, it is 11 p.m. in
Sydney, Australia. Time zones
are adjusted to regional
administrative boundaries.

KEY TO MAP

⬤ MINUS HOURS

⬤ PLUS HOURS

○ GREENWICH MEAN TIME

◐ DATE LINE

▦ TIME ZONES

GMT
Greenwich Mean Time (GMT) is the time in Greenwich, England. Clocks are set depending on whether they are east or west of Greenwich.

INTERNATIONAL DATE LINE
The International Date Line is an imaginary line that runs along the 180° meridian but deviates around countries.

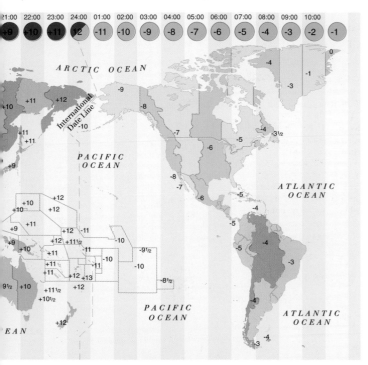

NORTH AMERICA

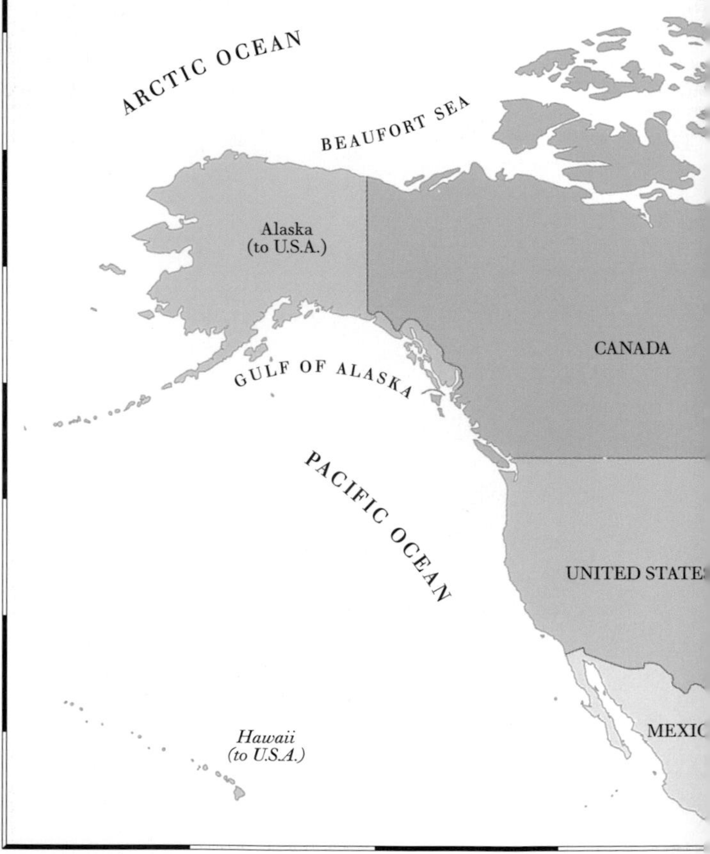

ARCTIC OCEAN

BEAUFORT SEA

Alaska
(to U.S.A.)

CANADA

GULF OF ALASKA

PACIFIC OCEAN

UNITED STATE

Hawaii
(to U.S.A.)

MEXIC

Greenland
(to Denmark)

BAFFIN BAY

HUDSON
BAY

LABRADOR SEA

ATLANTIC OCEAN

AMERICA

GULF OF
MEXICO

NORTH AMERICA

Canada and the United States of America
make up most of the continent. To the
south of the United States lie Mexico and
Central America. The northernmost part
of the continent sits in the Arctic Circle.
Greenland, to the northeast of Canada, is
the largest island in the world.

ALASKA AND
WESTERN CANADA

AT THE END OF the last ice age, people
travelled from Asia into North America
over the Bering landbridge, which
connected the
continents at
present-day
Alaska.

ARCTIC OCEAN

Bering Strait

BROOKS RANGE

Prudhoe Bay

BEAUFO

St. Lawrence I.

Nunivak I.

Yukon

St. Matthew I.

ALASKA
(U.S.A.)

Porcupine

BERING SEA

Fairbanks

Yukon

YUKON TERRITORY

Umnak I.
Unalaska I.
Unimak I.

Bristol Bay

ALASKA RANGE

Dawson

Anchorage

ALASKA
P 550,043
L English

Kodiak I.

Gulf of Alaska

WHITEHORSE

ROCKY MOUN

PACIFIC

JUNEAU

INDUSTRY
Fishing, oil, minerals, timber.
Railways were the key to the
development of farming in western
Canada. The U.S.A.'s biggest oil
field is at Prudhoe Bay, Alaska.

CLIMATE
A polar climate prevails
in the north; the south is warmer.
The Pacific coast, near Vancouver,
has the warmest winters, and
temperatures rarely fall below freezing.

Queen
Charlotte Is.

OCEAN

HISTORY
The U.S.A.
bought Alaska from
Russia in 1867 for
$7.2 million. Many
Americans thought this
was a waste of money until
gold was discovered there
in 1896 and oil in 1968.

BRITI
COLUMBI

Vancouver I.

Vancou

VICTOR

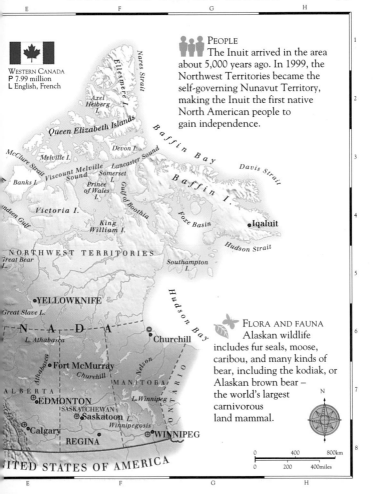

WESTERN CANADA
P 7.99 million
L English, French

PEOPLE

The Inuit arrived in the area about 5,000 years ago. In 1999, the Northwest Territories became the self-governing Nunavut Territory, making the Inuit the first native North American people to gain independence.

FLORA AND FAUNA

Alaskan wildlife includes fur seals, moose, caribou, and many kinds of bear, including the kodiak, or Alaskan brown bear – the world's largest carnivorous land mammal.

EASTERN CANADA

ALTHOUGH IT IS the second largest country in the world, Canada has a relatively small population. Most people live within 160 km (100 miles) of the U.S. border. Snowbound for most of the year, the Hudson Bay area is a wilderness of forests, rivers, and lakes.

PEOPLE
The Vikings were the first Europeans to visit eastern Canada in about 986 B.C. They settled for only a short time before the Native Americans drove them away.

INDUSTRY
Wood industries, oil, zinc, nickel, hydro-electricity, uranium. The area off the east coast called the Grand Banks is one of the world's richest fishing areas. Newsprint, made from wood pulp, is a major export from the Atlantic provinces.

Salisbur
Nottingham I.
Mansel I.

Inukjuak

H u d s o n   B a y

Belcher Is.

C. Henrietta Maria

MANITOBA

Winisk

Severn

James Bay

Attawapiskat

Attawapiskat

O N T A R I O

Albany

C A N

Lake of the Woods

L. Nipigon

Thunder Bay

Timmins

UNITED

Lake Superior

STATES OF

Sault
Sainte Marie

Ottawa

Sudbury

AMERICA

Lake Michigan

Lake Huron

TORONTO

Hamilton

Lal
Ontar

London

Niagar
Falls

Windsor

L. Erie

UNIT

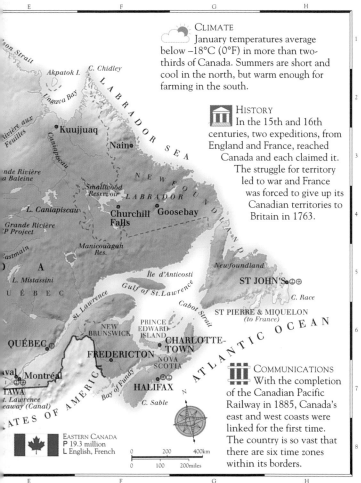

CLIMATE
January temperatures average below –18°C (0°F) in more than two-thirds of Canada. Summers are short and cool in the north, but warm enough for farming in the south.

HISTORY
In the 15th and 16th centuries, two expeditions, from England and France, reached Canada and each claimed it. The struggle for territory led to war and France was forced to give up its Canadian territories to Britain in 1763.

COMMUNICATIONS
With the completion of the Canadian Pacific Railway in 1885, Canada's east and west coasts were linked for the first time. The country is so vast that there are six time zones within its borders.

Hudson Strait
Akpatok I.
C. Chidley
Ungava Bay
LABRADOR SEA
Rivière aux Feuilles
Kuujjuaq
Nain
Caniapiscau
NEWFOUNDLAND
Grande Rivière la Baleine
Smallwood Reservoir
LABRADOR
L. Caniapiscau
Churchill Falls
Goosebay
Grande Ricière JP Project
Manicouagan Res.
Eastmain
L. Mistassini
Newfoundland
QUÉBEC
Île d'Anticosti
ST JOHN'S ⊕⊕
Gulf of St.Lawrence
C. Race
St.Lawrence
Cabot Strait
ST PIERRE & MIQUELON (to France)
QUÉBEC
NEW BRUNSWICK
PRINCE EDWARD ISLAND
CHARLOTTE-TOWN
ATLANTIC OCEAN
aval
Montréal
FREDERICTON
NOVA SCOTIA
TAWA
St. Lawrence Seaway (Canal)
HALIFAX
Bay of Fundy
C. Sable
TATES OF AMERIC

EASTERN CANADA
P 19.3 million
L English, French

0   200   400km
0   100   200miles

NORTHEASTERN STATES

WITH ITS RICH MINERAL resources and safe harbours, northeast America was the first area on the continent to be colonized by Europeans. In 1620, English pilgrims sailed on the *Mayflower* to settle in a region that is still called New England. During the mid-19th century, European immigrants settled in New York City and in other East Coast cities. Today, this region is the most densely populated and heavily industrialized area of the U.S.A.

CLIMATE
This area of the U.S.A. has a temperate climate, with warm and humid summers. However, the northeastern region, in particular, can experience very heavy snowfall from November to April.

NORTHEASTERN STATES
P 51.5 million
L English

PEOPLE
Northeastern Native American tribes, such as the Wampanoag, the Algonquin, and the tribes of the Iroquois League, were the first to come into contact with European settlers and explorers.

INDUSTRY
Oil, iron, steel, chemicals, maple sugar, blueberries, cranberries, fishing, tourism. Vermont is the main producer of maple syrup in the U.S.A. The stock exchange on Wall Street, New York City, is the largest in the world.

Niaga
Fal

Lake Erie Buffa

Erie

OHIO

PENNSYLVAN

Pittsburgh

WEST
VIRGINIA

APPALACHI
MTS

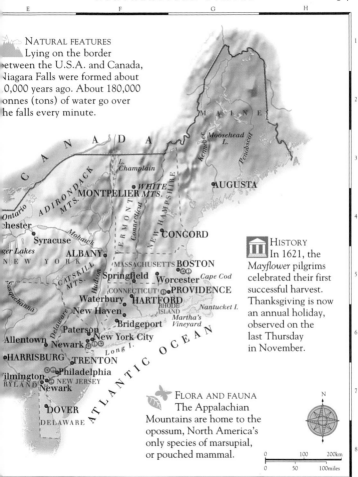

NATURAL FEATURES
Lying on the border
between the U.S.A. and Canada,
Niagara Falls were formed about
10,000 years ago. About 180,000
tonnes (tons) of water go over
the falls every minute.

HISTORY
In 1621, the
Mayflower pilgrims
celebrated their first
successful harvest.
Thanksgiving is now
an annual holiday,
observed on the
last Thursday
in November.

FLORA AND FAUNA
The Appalachian
Mountains are home to the
opossum, North America's
only species of marsupial,
or pouched mammal.

Map labels:

CANADA

L. Champlain

Mooshead L.

Kennebec

Penobscot

MAINE

ADIRONDACK MTS.

WHITE MTS.

MONTPELIER

AUGUSTA

VERMONT

NEW HAMPSHIRE

Ontario

chester

Mohawk

Syracuse

ALBANY

CONCORD

ger Lakes

NEW YORK

CATSKILL MTS.

MASSACHUSETTS   BOSTON

Springfield   Worcester   Cape Cod

Susquehanna

Hudson

Connecticut

CONNECTICUT

PROVIDENCE

Waterbury   HARTFORD

New Haven

RHODE ISLAND

Nantucket I.

Bridgeport

Martha's Vineyard

Delaware

Paterson   New York City

Allentown   Newark

Long I.

HARRISBURG   TRENTON

ilmington   Philadelphia

RYLAND   Newark

NEW JERSEY

ATLANTIC OCEAN

DOVER

DELAWARE

N

0   100   200km
0   50   100miles

SOUTHERN STATES

BY THE 19TH CENTURY, the wealth of the South was based on crops like tobacco, indigo, rice, and especially cotton, which was grown on large plantations by African slaves. The area is known today for New Orleans' jazz, Florida's Disney World, and the Kentucky Derby. The city of Washington, in the District of Columbia, was made the U.S. capital in 1800.

CLIMATE
Summers are long and hot; winters are mild, but temperatures are generally warmer on the coast than inland. Southern Florida is tropical.

INDUSTRY
Soya beans, coal, peanuts, cotton, citrus fruits, tobacco, oil, tourism. Georgia grows half of the U.S.A's peanuts – most are used to make peanut butter.

THE ARTS
The French brought Mardi Gras to America in the early 1700s Celebrated in many of the southern states, the most famous festival is held in New Orleans. Here parades last for a week before Mardi Gras Day, the day before Lent starts.

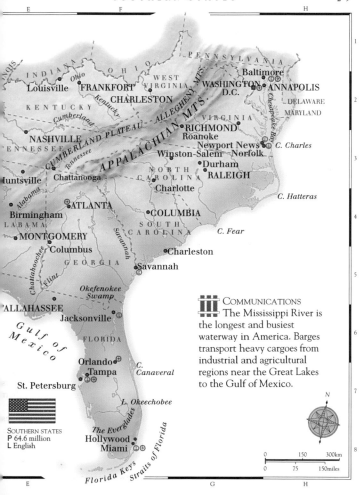

E | F | H

1

PENNSYLVANIA

INDIANA OHIO WEST **Baltimore**
Louisville **FRANKFORT** VIRGINIA **WASHINGTON** **ANNAPOLIS**
Ohio **CHARLESTON** D.C. DELAWARE

KENTUCKY *Kentucky* VIRGINIA MARYLAND
Cumberland

NASHVILLE APPALACHIAN MTS. **RICHMOND**
ENNESSEE *Tennessee* Roanoke
Newport News C. Charles
Winston-Salem Norfolk
CUMBERLAND PLATEAU ALLEGHENY MTS.

luntsville Chattanooga NORTH •Durham
CAROLINA **RALEIGH**

Charlotte

•ATLANTA •COLUMBIA C. Hatteras
Birmingham SOUTH
LABAMA CAROLINA C. Fear
LABAMA •MONTGOMERY
Columbus
GEORGIA •Charleston
Chattahoochee •Savannah
Flint

Okefenokee
Swamp

ALLAHASSEE
Jacksonville

Gulf of FLORIDA
Mexico

Orlando•
•Tampa C.
Canaveral
St. Petersburg

L. Okeechobee

The Everglades
Hollywood
Miami

Florida Keys *Straits of Florida*

SOUTHERN STATES
P 64.6 million
L English

III COMMUNICATIONS
The Mississippi River is
the longest and busiest
waterway in America. Barges
transport heavy cargoes from
industrial and agricultural
regions near the Great Lakes
to the Gulf of Mexico.

N

0   150   300km
0   75   150miles

E | G | H

THE GREAT LAKES

THE STATES OF Indiana, Illinois, Michigan, Ohio, Wisconsin, and Minnesota, which all border on one or more of the five Great Lakes, are often called the industrial and agricultural heartland of the United States. The region is rich in natural resources, with large areas of fertile farmland on flat plains called prairies.

CLIMATE
The region around the Great Lakes has warm summers but quite severe winters, and parts of the lakes can freeze over. Minnesota, in particular, suffers from heavy snowstorms.

ENVIRONMENT
The Great Lakes – Ontario, Huron, Superior, Michigan, and Erie – together form the largest area of fresh water in the world. Heavy industry has caused severe water pollution, and in some areas it is dangerous to eat the fish or swim.

GREAT LAKES STATES
P 46.4 million
L English

INDUSTRY
Vehicles, coal, iron, grain, maize, cherries. Nearly half of the world's maize crop and a third of the cherry crop are grown in the Great Lakes region. Detroit is known as "motor city" because it is the centre of the U.S. car industry.

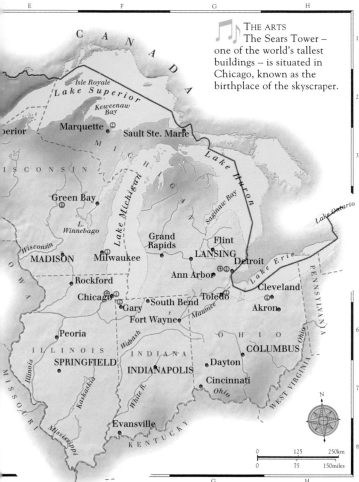

♫♪ THE ARTS
The Sears Tower –
one of the world's tallest
buildings – is situated in
Chicago, known as the
birthplace of the skyscraper.

CANADA

Lake Superior

Isle Royale

Keweenaw Bay

Superior

Marquette

Sault Ste. Marie

Lake Huron

MICHIGAN

WISCONSIN

Green Bay

L. Winnebago

Lake Michigan

Saginaw Bay

Lake Ontario

Wisconsin

MADISON

Milwaukee

Grand Rapids

Flint

LANSING

Detroit

Lake Erie

IOWA

Rockford

Ann Arbor

Cleveland

PENNSYLVANIA

Chicago

Gary

South Bend

Toledo

Akron

Fort Wayne

Maumee

Peoria

Wabash

OHIO

COLUMBUS

ILLINOIS

INDIANA

Ohio

WEST VIRGINIA

SPRINGFIELD

Kaskaskia

INDIANAPOLIS

Dayton

Cincinnati

MISSOURI

White R.

Ohio

Mississippi

Evansville

KENTUCKY

N

0 125 250km

0 75 150miles

G H

CENTRAL AND MOUNTAIN STATES

THE GREAT Plains, the Rocky Mountains, and the Mississippi lowlands dominate the landscape of the Midwest. Once home to Native Americans and herds of bison, the Great Plains were settled in the 19th century by Europeans, who forced the Native Americans onto reservations and slaughtered the bison to near extinction.

HISTORY

Pioneers travelling to the West had to cross the Great Plains, which were known as the "Great American Desert". The last area to be settled, it is now a wealthy agricultural region.

CENTRAL AND
MOUNTAIN STATES
P 18.7 million
L English

CLIMATE

West of the Rockies, the summers are cooler and the winters are warmer. States on the Great Plains have an extreme climate, which can change quite suddenly and violently – blizzards, hail, thunderstorms, and tornadoes may occur.

NATURAL FEATURES

The Rocky Mountains extend through Canada and the U.S.A. for more than 4,800 km (3,000 miles). They divide North America and separate the rivers flowing west to the Pacific from those flowing east to the Atlantic.

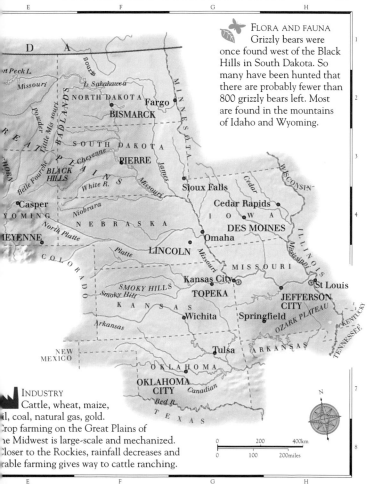

FLORA AND FAUNA
Grizzly bears were
once found west of the Black
Hills in South Dakota. So
many have been hunted that
there are probably fewer than
800 grizzly bears left. Most
are found in the mountains
of Idaho and Wyoming.

INDUSTRY
Cattle, wheat, maize,
il, coal, natural gas, gold.
Crop farming on the Great Plains of
he Midwest is large-scale and mechanized.
Closer to the Rockies, rainfall decreases and
rable farming gives way to cattle ranching.

0   200   400km
0   100   200miles

SOUTHWESTERN STATES

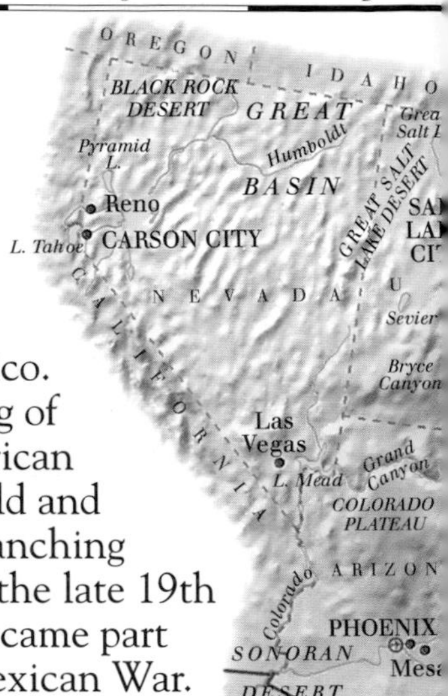

THE FIRST Europeans in the Southwest were the Spanish, who travelled north from Mexico. This resulted in a mingling of Spanish and Native American cultures in the region. Gold and silver mining and cattle-ranching attracted other settlers in the late 19th century, when this area became part of the U.S.A. after the Mexican War.

NATURAL FEATURES

The Colorado plateau has some unusual landforms, including natural bridges and arches of solid rock. Over the past million years, the Colorado River has cut away the plateau, forming the world's largest river gorge – the Grand Canyon.

HISTORY

At the end of the Mexican War (1846–48), the U.S.A. acquired Utah, Nevada, California, and parts of Arizona, New Mexico, Colorado, and Wyoming. One of the causes of the war was a border dispute between Texas and Mexico.

SOUTHWESTERN STATES
P 28.4 million
L English

PEOPLE

Some of the earliest Native Americans lived in the Nevada area. Bones and ashes discovered near Las Vegas indicate that people may have lived there more than 20,000 years ago. Today, the region has the largest concentration of Native Americans in the country.

Map labels: OREGON · IDAHO · BLACK ROCK DESERT · GREAT · Grea[t] · Salt L[ake] · Pyramid L. · Humboldt · BASIN · Reno · GREAT SALT LAKE DESERT · SA · L. Tahoe · CARSON CITY · LA · CI · NEVADA · U · Sevier · Bryce Canyon · Las Vegas · L. Mead · Grand Canyon · COLORADO PLATEAU · ARIZONA · Colorado · PHOENIX · SONORAN · Mesa · DESERT · Tucso[n]

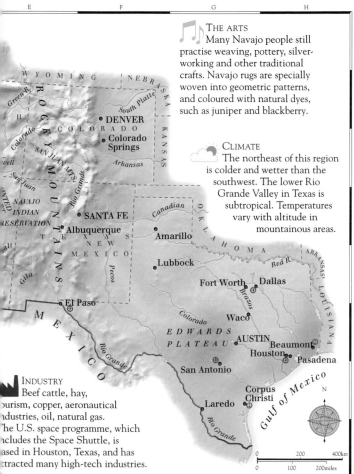

THE ARTS
Many Navajo people still practise weaving, pottery, silver-working and other traditional crafts. Navajo rugs are specially woven into geometric patterns, and coloured with natural dyes, such as juniper and blackberry.

CLIMATE
The northeast of this region is colder and wetter than the southwest. The lower Rio Grande Valley in Texas is subtropical. Temperatures vary with altitude in mountainous areas.

INDUSTRY
Beef cattle, hay, tourism, copper, aeronautical industries, oil, natural gas. The U.S. space programme, which includes the Space Shuttle, is based in Houston, Texas, and has attracted many high-tech industries.

PACIFIC STATES

ALL THREE STATES on the West Coast are major agricultural producers – Washington and Oregon supply one-third of the softwood timber in the U.S. and California produces half of the country's fruit and vegetables. Situated where two of the Earth's plates meet, the area suffers from earthquakes and volcanic activity. Mount St. Helens, dormant since 1857, erupted in 1980, losing some 400 m (1,300 ft) off its height.

NATURAL FEATURES
The lowest point in the western hemisphere is in Death Valley, 86 m (282 ft) below sea level. One of the driest, hottest places on Earth, the highest temperature, 57°C (135°F), was recorded there in 1913, and its average rainfall is only 38 mm (1.5 in) per year.

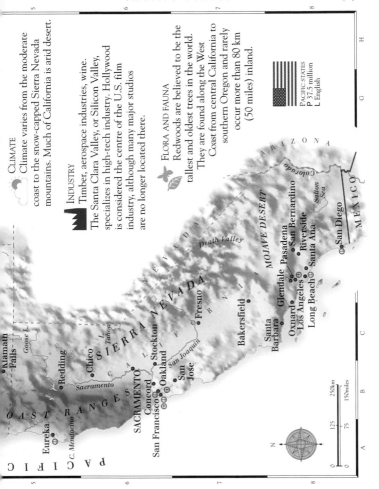

CLIMATE
Climate varies from the moderate coast to the snow-capped Sierra Nevada mountains. Much of California is arid desert.

INDUSTRY
Timber, aerospace industries, wine. The Santa Clara Valley, or Silicon Valley, specializes in high-tech industry. Hollywood is considered the centre of the U.S. film industry, although many major studios are no longer located there.

FLORA AND FAUNA
Redwoods are believed to be the tallest and oldest trees in the world. They are found along the West Coast from central California to southern Oregon and rarely occur more than 80 km (50 miles) inland.

PACIFIC STATES
P 37.5 million
L English

A R I Z O N A

Colorado

MEXICO

Salton Sea

San Diego

San Bernardino

Riverside

Pasadena

Glendale

Santa Ana

Oxnard

Los Angeles

Long Beach

MOJAVE DESERT

Santa Barbara

Death Valley

N E V A D A

S I E R R A   N E V A D A

Bakersfield

Fresno

San Joaquin

C A L I F O R N I A

Stockton

San Jose

Oakland

Concord

San Francisco

SACRAMENTO

Sacramento

L. Tahoe

Chico

Redding

Goose L.

Klamath Falls

C O A S T   R A N G E S

C. Mendocino

Eureka

P A C I F I C

250km

150miles

125

75

0

0

N

MEXICO

THE ANCIENT empires of the Maya and Aztec flourished for centuries before the Spanish invaded Mexico in 1519, lured there by legends of hoards of gold and silver. Mexico gained its independence in 1810, after 300 years of Spanish rule. Today, most Mexicans are *mestizo*, a mix of Spanish and Native American. Although Spanish is the official language, Native American languages such as Maya, Nahuatl, and Zapotec are also widely spoken.

Map labels:
UNITED STATES
Tijuana
Mexicali
Nogales
Ángel de la Guarda I.
Hermosillo
BAJA CALIFORNIA
Cedros I.
Tiburón I.
Gulf of California
SIERRA MADRE
Culiacá
La Paz

CLIMATE
The Mexican plateau and mountains are warm for most of the year. The Pacific coast has a tropical climate.

MEXICO
P 90 million
L Spanish

FLORA AND FAUNA
The Mexican beaded lizard and the gila monster are the only two poisonous lizards known. The largest of all cacti is the giant saguaro, which grows in the Sonora Desert to a height of more than 18 m (60 ft).

NATURAL FEATURES
The plateau of Mexico is enclosed to the west and east by the Sierra Madre mountain ranges, which occupy 75 per cent of the total land area. Mexico is so mountainous and arid in parts that only 12 per cent of the land is arable.

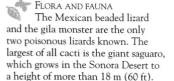

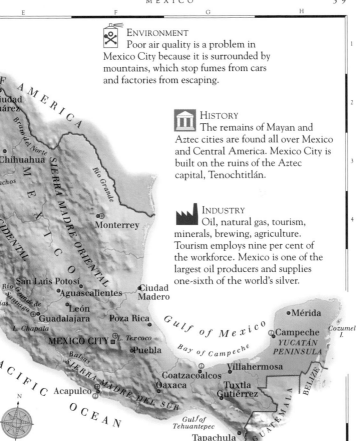

ENVIRONMENT
Poor air quality is a problem in Mexico City because it is surrounded by mountains, which stop fumes from cars and factories from escaping.

HISTORY
The remains of Mayan and Aztec cities are found all over Mexico and Central America. Mexico City is built on the ruins of the Aztec capital, Tenochtitlán.

INDUSTRY
Oil, natural gas, tourism, minerals, brewing, agriculture. Tourism employs nine per cent of the workforce. Mexico is one of the largest oil producers and supplies one-sixth of the world's silver.

Map labels:

Ciudad Juárez
Chihuahua
Monterrey
San Luis Potosí
Aguascalientes
León
Guadalajara
Poza Rica
Ciudad Madero
MEXICO CITY
Puebla
Acapulco
Oaxaca
Coatzacoalcos
Villahermosa
Tuxtla Gutiérrez
Tapachula
Mérida
Campeche
Cozumel I.

AMERICA
SIERRA MADRE OCCIDENTAL
SIERRA MADRE ORIENTAL
MEXICO
SIERRA MADRE DEL SUR
YUCATÁN PENINSULA
BELIZE
GUATEMALA

Bravo del Norte
Río Grande
Conchos
Río Grande de Santiago
L. Chapala
L. Texcoco
Balsas

Gulf of Mexico
Bay of Campeche
PACIFIC OCEAN
Gulf of Tehuantepec

N

0   200   400km
0   100   200miles

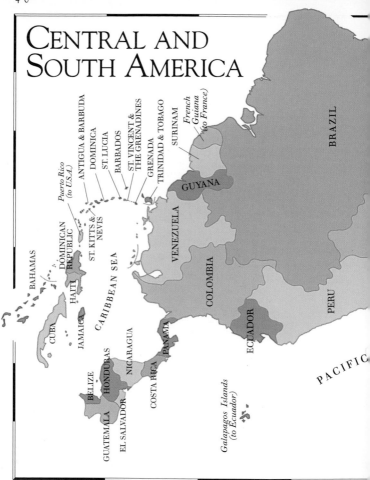

CENTRAL AND SOUTH AMERICA

BRAZIL

*Puerto Rico
(to U.S.A.)*

ANTIGUA & BARBUDA

DOMINICA

ST. LUCIA

BARBADOS

ST. VINCENT &
THE GRENADINES

GRENADA

TRINIDAD & TOBAGO

SURINAM

*French
Guiana
(to France)*

GUYANA

VENEZUELA

COLOMBIA

PERU

ST. KITTS &
NEVIS

DOMINICAN
REPUBLIC

HAITI

BAHAMAS

CUBA

JAMAICA

CARIBBEAN SEA

ECUADOR

PANAMA

NICARAGUA

COSTA RICA

BELIZE

HONDURAS

GUATEMALA

EL SALVADOR

*Galapagos Islands
(to Ecuador)*

PACIFIC

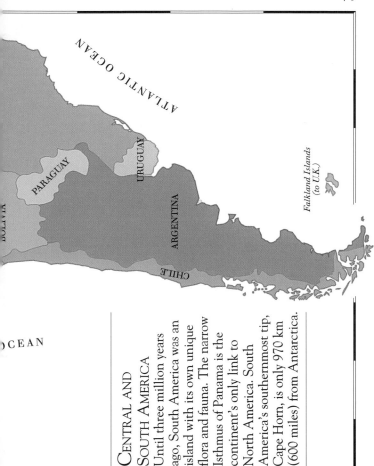

ATLANTIC OCEAN

BOLIVIA

PARAGUAY

URUGUAY

ARGENTINA

CHILE

Falkland Islands
(to U.K.)

OCEAN

CENTRAL AND SOUTH AMERICA

Until three million years ago, South America was an island with its own unique flora and fauna. The narrow Isthmus of Panama is the continent's only link to North America. South America's southernmost tip, Cape Horn, is only 970 km (600 miles) from Antarctica.

CENTRAL AMERICA AND THE CARIBBEAN

CENTRAL AMERICA FORMS a narrow land bridge linking North and South America. To the east lie the Caribbean islands, many of which are uninhabited.

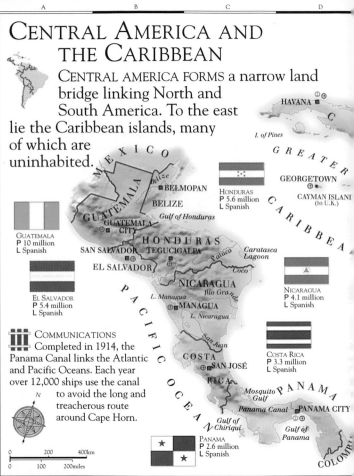

HAVANA

I. of Pines

GREATER

MEXICO

Belize

■ BELMOPAN

GEORGETOWN

HONDURAS
P 5.6 million
L Spanish

CAYMAN ISLANDS
(to U.K.)

BELIZE

Gulf of Honduras

CARIBBEAN

GUATEMALA
⊕■ GUATEMALA CITY

HONDURAS

GUATEMALA
P 10 million
L Spanish

SAN SALVADOR ⊕ TEGUCIGALPA ⊕

Patuca

Caratasca Lagoon

■ EL SALVADOR

NICARAGUA
Rio Grande

Coco

EL SALVADOR
P 5.4 million
L Spanish

NICARAGUA
L. Managua
⊕■ MANAGUA
L. Nicaragua

NICARAGUA
P 4.1 million
L Spanish

PACIFIC

San Juan

COMMUNICATIONS
Completed in 1914, the Panama Canal links the Atlantic and Pacific Oceans. Each year over 12,000 ships use the canal to avoid the long and treacherous route around Cape Horn.

COSTA RICA
⊕■ SAN JOSÉ

COSTA RICA
P 3.3 million
L Spanish

OCEAN

Mosquito Gulf

PANAMA

N

Panama Canal ■ PANAMA CITY

Gulf of Chiriqui

Gulf of Panama

| 0 | 200 | 400km |
| 0 | 100 | 200miles |

PANAMA
P 2.6 million
L Spanish

COLOMBIA

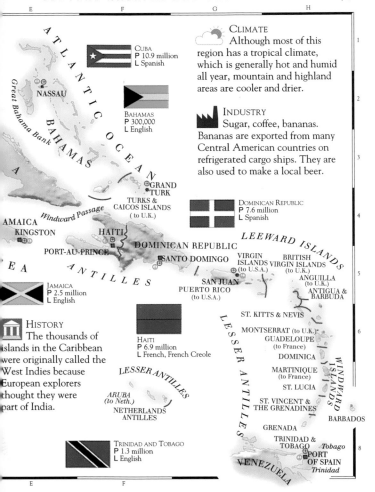

CUBA
P 10.9 million
L Spanish

Great Bahama Bank

NASSAU

BAHAMAS
P 300,000
L English

GRAND
TURK

TURKS &
CAICOS ISLANDS
(to U.K.)

Windward Passage

AMAICA
KINGSTON

HAITI

PORT-AU-PRINCE

DOMINICAN REPUBLIC

SANTO DOMINGO

LEEWARD ISLANDS

DOMINICAN REPUBLIC
P 7.6 million
L Spanish

JAMAICA
P 2.5 million
L English

VIRGIN
ISLANDS
(to U.S.A.)

BRITISH
VIRGIN ISLANDS
(to U.K.)

SAN JUAN
PUERTO RICO
(to U.S.A.)

ANGUILLA
(to U.K.)

ANTIGUA &
BARBUDA

ST. KITTS & NEVIS

HAITI
P 6.9 million
L French, French Creole

MONTSERRAT (to U.K.)

GUADELOUPE
(to France)

DOMINICA

MARTINIQUE
(to France)

ST. LUCIA

ST. VINCENT &
THE GRENADINES

LESSER ANTILLES

ARUBA
(to Neth.)

NETHERLANDS
ANTILLES

WINDWARD ISLANDS

BARBADOS

GRENADA

TRINIDAD AND TOBAGO
P 1.3 million
L English

TRINIDAD &
TOBAGO   *Tobago*

PORT
OF SPAIN

Trinidad

VENEZUELA

CLIMATE
Although most of this
region has a tropical climate,
which is generally hot and humid
all year, mountain and highland
areas are cooler and drier.

INDUSTRY
Sugar, coffee, bananas.
Bananas are exported from many
Central American countries on
refrigerated cargo ships. They are
also used to make a local beer.

HISTORY
The thousands of
islands in the Caribbean
were originally called the
West Indies because
European explorers
thought they were
part of India.

Northern South America

THE INCAS RULED MUCH of this area in the 15th century, and today large numbers of their descendants live in Peru, Ecuador, and Bolivia. In 1533, the last Incan emperor was executed by the Spanish, who colonized this region. The French, Dutch, and British later settled in the countries east of Venezuela, although all but French Guiana are now independent.

VENEZUELA
P 20.6 million
L Spanish

GUYANA
P 800,000
L English

SURINAM
P 400,000
L Dutch

CARIBBEAN SEA

Gulf of Venezuela

Margarita I.

Barranquilla
Cartagena
Gulf of Darien

Santa Marta
Maracaibo
L. Maracaibo
Barquisimeto
Valencia
CARACAS
Cumaná
Maturín
Ciudad Bolívar
Ciudad Guayana

PANAMA

Medellín
Magdalena
Cauca
Barinas
Mérida
Arauca
Apure
Orinoco

BOGOTÁ
Buenaventura
Cali
Villavicencio
Meta
Guaviare

COLOMBIA
VENEZUELA
GUYANA
SURINAM
FRENCH GUIANA
(to France)

GEORGETOWN
New Amsterdam
PARAMARIBO
CAYENNE

Essequibo
Berbice
Courantyne
Marowijne

AMAZON BASIN

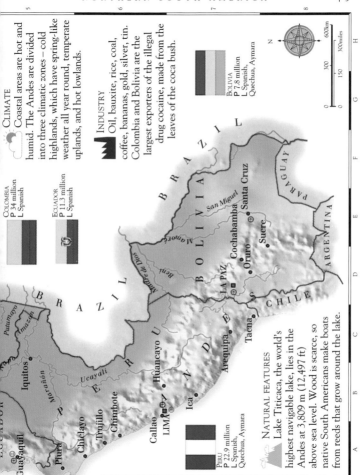

CLIMATE

Coastal areas are hot and humid. The Andes are divided into three climatic zones – cold highlands, which have spring-like weather all year round, temperate uplands, and hot lowlands.

INDUSTRY

Oil, bauxite, rice, coal, coffee, bananas, gold, silver, tin. Colombia and Bolivia are the largest exporters of the illegal drug cocaine, made from the leaves of the coca bush.

COLOMBIA
P 34 million
L Spanish

ECUADOR
P 11.3 million
L Spanish

BOLIVIA
P 7.8 million
L Spanish,
Quechua, Aymara

PERU
P 22.9 million
L Spanish,
Quechua, Aymara

NATURAL FEATURES

Lake Titicaca, the world's highest navigable lake, lies in the Andes at 3,809 m (12,497 ft) above sea level. Wood is scarce, so native South Americans make boats from the reeds that grow around the lake.

BRAZIL
BOLIVIA
PARAGUAY
ARGENTINA
CHILE
PERU
ECUADOR

LA PAZ
Oruro
Cochabamba
Sucre
Santa Cruz
San Miguel
Mamoré
Beni
Madre de Dios
Ucayali
Marañón
Amazon
Putumayo
Iquitos
Guayaquil
Piura
Chiclayo
Trujillo
Chimbote
Huancayo
Callao
LIMA
Ica
Arequipa
Tacna

BRAZIL

OCCUPYING NEARLY HALF of South America, Brazil has the largest river basin in the world. Many Brazilians are descendants of Portuguese, who colonized Brazil in the 16th century, and Africans, who were brought to work on sugar plantations. Over the years, people have moved from the countryside in search of work, so that today almost 75 per cent of Brazilians live in cities. Chronic housing shortages mean about 25 million people live in sprawling shanty towns called *favelas*.

PEOPLE

There were once about two million indigenous people living in Amazonia. Today only 50,000 remain. The survival of many tribes and their way of life is threatened by the destruction of the Amazon rainforest.

ATLANTIC OCEAN

Natal

Fortaleza

Teresina

São Luís

Parnaíba

Belém

SERRA PELADA

Xingu

Santarém

Amazon

FRENCH GUIANA (to France)

SURINAM

GUYANA

Balbina Res.

Manaus

Madeira

Tapajós

Purus

VENEZUELA

Negro

Amazon

B R A Z I L

AMAZON BASIN

COLOMBIA

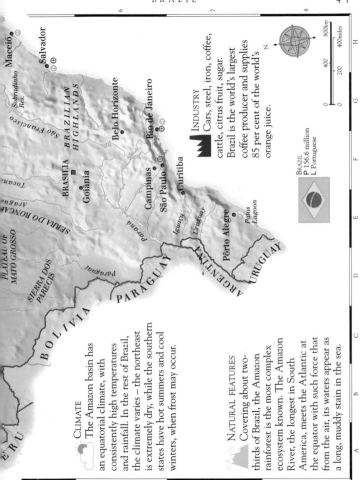

CLIMATE
The Amazon basin has an equatorial climate, with consistently high temperatures and rainfall. In the rest of Brazil, the climate varies – the northeast is extremely dry, while the southern states have hot summers and cool winters, when frost may occur.

NATURAL FEATURES
Covering about two-thirds of Brazil, the Amazon rainforest is the most complex ecosystem known. The Amazon River, the longest in South America, meets the Atlantic at the equator with such force that from the air, its waters appear as a long, muddy stain in the sea.

INDUSTRY
Cars, steel, iron, coffee, cattle, citrus fruit, sugar. Brazil is the world's largest coffee producer and supplies 85 per cent of the world's orange juice.

BRAZIL
P 156.6 million
L Portuguese

SOUTHERN SOUTH AMERICA

THE LANDSCAPE of this region of South America varies from snow-capped volcanoes in the Andes to the wastelands of Patagonia. In the heart of Argentina lie the Pampas, fertile grasslands where vast herds of cattle graze. In parts, grasses grow up to 3 m (10 ft) high. Chile is separated from the rest of the region by the Andes, which run the length of the continent.

CLIMATE

Paraguay is subtropical; farther south is temperate. The Andes have year-round snow, while parts of the Atacama desert in Chile have had no rain for 400 years.

URUGUAY
P 3.1 million
L Spanish

PARAGUAY
P 4.5 million
L Spanish,
Guaraní

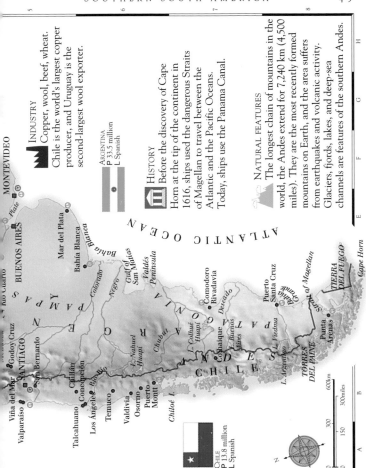

INDUSTRY

Copper, wool, beef, wheat. Chile is the world's largest copper producer, and Uruguay is the second-largest wool exporter.

ARGENTINA
P 33.5 million
L Spanish

HISTORY

Before the discovery of Cape Horn at the tip of the continent in 1616, ships used the dangerous Straits of Magellan to travel between the Atlantic and the Pacific Oceans. Today, ships use the Panama Canal.

NATURAL FEATURES

The longest chain of mountains in the world, the Andes extend for 7,240 km (4,500 miles). They are the most recently formed mountains on Earth, and the area suffers from earthquakes and volcanic activity. Glaciers, fjords, lakes, and deep-sea channels are features of the southern Andes.

CHILE
P 13.8 million
L Spanish

ATLANTIC OCEAN

MONTEVIDEO
Plate
BUENOS AIRES
Mar del Plata
Bahía Blanca
Gulf of San Matías
Valdés Peninsula
Colorado
Negro
P A M P A S
Río Cuarto
Godoy Cruz
SANTIAGO
San Bernardo
Viña del Mar
Valparaíso
Chillán
Concepción
Talcahuano
Los Ángeles
Bío-Bío
Temuco
Valdivia
Osorno
Puerto Montt
Chiloé I.
L. Nahuel Huapi
Chubut
L. Colhué Huapi
Comodoro Rivadavia
Deseado
P A T A G O N I A
Coihaique
L. Buenos Aires
Puerto Santa Cruz
Santa Cruz
A N D E S
C H I L E
L. Viedma
L. Argentino
TORRES DEL PAINE
Punta Arenas
Strait of Magellan
Grande
TIERRA DEL FUEGO
Cape Horn

600km
300miles
300
150
0

N

THE ANTARCTIC

CONTAINING 80 PERCENT of the world's freshwater, the continent of Antarctica lies buried under ice more than 2 km (1.2 miles) thick. The surrounding seas are partly frozen, and icebergs barricade over 90 percent of the coastline.

ATLANTIC OCEAN

INDIAN OCEAN

South Orkney Is. (to U.K.)

SCOTIA SEA

Elephant I. (to U.K.)

South Shetland Is. (to U.K.)

ANTARCTIC PENINSULA

QUEEN MAUD LAND

ENDERBY LAND

Lutzow-Holm Bay

Drake Passage

Anvers I. (to U.S.A.)

WEDDELL SEA

PALMER LAND

C. Darnl

Mackenz Bay

SOUTH POLAR PLATEAU

Peter the First I. (to Norway)

BELLINGSHAUSEN SEA

ELLSWORTH MTS.

South Pole

TRANSANTARCTIC MTS.

DAV SE

Vincen Bay

MARIE BYRD LAND

AMUNDSEN SEA

WILKES LAND

Porpoise Bay

PACIFIC OCEAN

C. Colbeck

ROSS SEA

C. Adare

Balleny Is.

FLORA AND FAUNA

Not many plants and animals can survive on land, although the surrounding seas teem with life. Despite the cold, few birds and sea creatures migrate to warmer waters.

CLIMATE

Powerful winds form a narrow storm belt that creates severe blizzards. Summer temperatures barely reach over freezing point, and in winter the temperature can fall to –80°C (–112°F).

ENVIRONMENT

Scientists estimate that the ozone hole emerged over Antarctica in 1980. Each spring, increased sunshine activates CFCs leading to rapid ozone depletion.

THE ARCTIC

A FROZEN OCEAN surrounded by land, the Arctic is covered by ice up to 30 m (98 ft) thick. Most of the surrounding tundra, or vast treeless plains, are permanently frozen.

RUSSIAN FEDERATION

ALASKA (U.S.A.)

CHUKCHI SEA

Pevek

Wrangel I. (to Russian Fed.)

EAST SIBERIAN SEA

Prudhoe Bay

BEAUFORT SEA

Limit of Permanent Pack Ice

New Siberian Is. (to Russian Fed.)

Tiksi

LAPTEV SEA

Banks I. (to Canada)

CANADA

Melville I. (to Canada)

TAYMYR PENINSULA

ARCTIC OCEAN

Queen Elizabeth Islands

Resolute

Limit of Permanent Pack Ice

Axel Heiberg I. (to Canada)

Devon I. (to Canada)

Ellesmere I. (to Canada)

North Pole

Severnaya Zemlya (to Russian Fed.)

Limit of Permanent Pack Ice

KARA SEA

Thule

Baffin I. (to Canada)

Franz Josef Land (to Russian Fed.)

Baffin Bay

KNUD RASMUSSEN LAND

BARENTS SEA

GREENLAND (to Denmark)

SVALBARD (to Norway)

Davis Strait

Godhavn

GREENLAND SEA

LONGYEARBYEN

Spitsbergen

GODTHÅB (NUUK)

Scoresbysund

Narssarsuaq

ATLANTIC OCEAN

C. Farvel

Denmark Strait

Jan Mayen (to Norway)

ICELAND

PEOPLE
The Inuit have lived in the Arctic Circle since 2500 B.C. Vikings arrived in A.D. 986.

ATLANTIC OCEAN

BENEATH THE WATERS of the Atlantic Ocean lies the Mid-Atlantic Ridge, one of the world's longest mountain chains. Some of its peaks are so high they form islands, such as the Azores. Apart from a wide rift-valley in the centre of the ridge, the ocean consists of vast featureless plains and is 8 km (5 miles) at its deepest point.

ICELAND
P 300,000
L Icelandic

CAPE VERDE
P 390,000
L Portuguese

EUROPE

BLACK SEA

Murmansk

BALTIC SEA

Bergen

Rotterdam

MEDITERRANEAN SEA

NORTH SEA

Aberdeen

GIBRALTAR

GREENLAND SEA

ARCTIC OCEAN

Denmark Strait

ICELAND
REYKJAVIK

Faeroe Islands (to Denmark)

GREENLAND

Azores (to Portugal)

Madeira (to Portugal)

Canary Islands

Mid-Atlantic Ridge

Davis Strait

Baffin Bay

LABRADOR SEA

C. Farewell (to Denmark)

Newfoundland

Grand Banks

Hudson Bay

NORTH AMERICA

St. Lawrence

New York City

Bermuda (to U.K.)

Mississippi

A

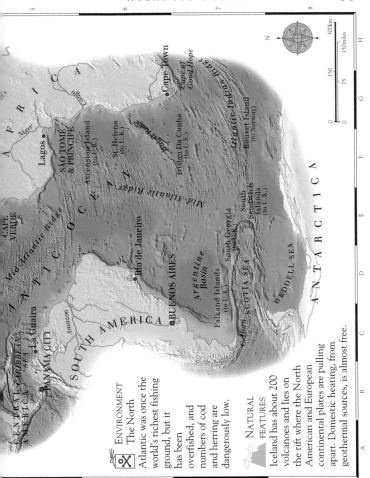

N
0 150 300km
0 75 150miles

AFRICA

Niger

Lagos

CAPE VERDE

Congo

Cape Town

Cape of Good Hope

SÃO TOMÉ & PRÍNCIPE

Ascension Island (to U.K.)

St. Helena (to U.K.)

Tristan Da Cunha (to U.K.)

Walvis Ridge

Mid-Atlantic Ridge

ATLANTIC

OCEAN

Mid-Atlantic Ridge

Atlantic-Indian Ridge

Bouvet Island (to Norway)

ANTARCTICA

PANAMA CITY

CENTRAL CARIBBEAN AMERICA SEA

La Guaira

SOUTH AMERICA

Amazon

Rio de Janeiro

BUENOS AIRES

Argentine Basin

Falkland Islands (to U.K.)

C. Horn

SCOTIA SEA

South Georgia (to U.K.)

South Sandwich Islands (to U.K.)

WEDDELL SEA

ANTARCTICA

ENVIRONMENT
The North
Atlantic was once the
world's richest fishing
ground, but it
has been
overfished, and
numbers of cod
and herring are
dangerously low.

NATURAL
FEATURES
Iceland has about 200
volcanoes and lies on
the rift where the North
American and European
continental plates are pulling
apart. Domestic heating, from
geothermal sources, is almost free.

EUROPE

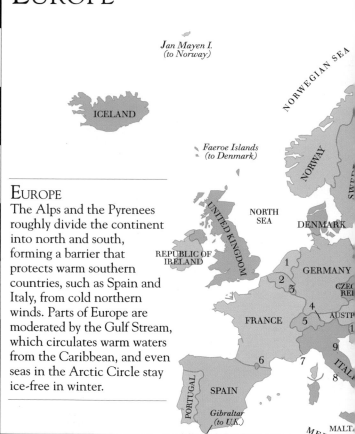

Jan Mayen I.
(to Norway)

ICELAND

Faeroe Islands
(to Denmark)

NORWEGIAN SEA

NORWAY

SWE

NORTH SEA

DENMARK

GERMANY

CZEC
REI

UNITED KINGDOM

REPUBLIC OF IRELAND

1

2

3

4

AUST

FRANCE

5

9

ITAL

6

7

8

PORTUGAL

SPAIN

Gibraltar
(to U.K.)

MALT
MEDITER

EUROPE

The Alps and the Pyrenees roughly divide the continent into north and south, forming a barrier that protects warm southern countries, such as Spain and Italy, from cold northern winds. Parts of Europe are moderated by the Gulf Stream, which circulates warm waters from the Caribbean, and even seas in the Arctic Circle stay ice-free in winter.

BARENTS SEA

FINLAND

BALTIC SEA

ESTONIA

LATVIA

LITHUANIA

BELORUSSIA

POLAND

SLOVAKIA

HUNGARY

RUSSIAN FEDERATION

UKRAINE

16

ROMANIA

BLACK SEA

BULGARIA

GEORGIA

2

13

14

15

AZERBAIJAN

ARMENIA

GREECE

MEDITERRANEAN SEA

1 NETHERLANDS
2 BELGIUM
3 LUXEMBOURG
4 LIECHTENSTEIN
5 SWITZERLAND
6 ANDORRA
7 MONACO
8 VATICAN CITY
9 SAN MARINO
10 SLOVENIA
11 CROATIA
12 BOSNIA/HERZEGOVINA
13 YUGOSLAVIA
14 MACEDONIA
15 ALBANIA
16 MOLDAVIA

SCANDINAVIA AND FINLAND

DURING PAST ICE AGES, much of Scandinavia and Finland were covered in glaciers that carved out the land, leaving steep-sided valleys, fjords, and lakes. The Finnish, originally from the east via Russia, differ from Scandinavians in culture and language.

FINLAND
P 5 million
L Finnish, Swedish

CLIMATE
Norway's west coast is warmed by the Gulf Stream. Northern temperatures fall to −30°C (−22°F) during the six-month winter; the south is milder.

INDUSTRY
Fishing, timber, wood-pulp, paper, oil, gas, car manufacture. Norway is western Europe's largest producer of oil.

NORWAY
P 4.2 million
L Norwegian

RUSSIAN FEDERATION

F I N L

Hammerfest

North Cape

L. Inari

Ounas

Ivalo

ARCTIC OCEAN

Oulu   *Oulu*

Torne

Muonio

Tromsø

L. Torne

L. Uldjiaur

Um

Lofoten Vesterålen

NORWEGIAN SEA

KJØLEN MTS

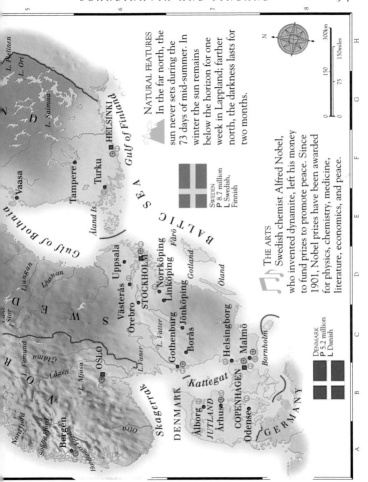

NATURAL FEATURES
In the far north, the sun never sets during the 73 days of mid-summer. In winter the sun remains below the horizon for one week in Lappland; farther north, the darkness lasts for two months.

SWEDEN
P 8.7 million
L Swedish, Finnish

THE ARTS
Swedish chemist Alfred Nobel, who invented dynamite, left his money to fund prizes to promote peace. Since 1901, Nobel prizes have been awarded for physics, chemistry, medicine, literature, economics, and peace.

DENMARK
P 5.2 million
L Danish

L. Puujinen
L. Ori
L. Saimaa
HELSINKI
Tampere
Turku
Gulf of Finland
Vaasa
Åland Is.
BALTIC SEA
Gulf of Bothnia
Ljungan
Ljusnan
Uppsala
Fårö
STOCKHOLM
Norrköping
Gottland
Västerås
Linköping
Örebro
L. Vättern
Öland
Lake Stor
Fermund
Gothenburg
Jönköping
L. Vänern
Borås
Glama
Lagen
Helsingborg
OSLO
Malmö
Bornholm
Bergen
COPENHAGEN
Kattegat
Skagerrak
Sognefjord
Nordfjord
Orra
Ålborg
JUTLAND
Århus
DENMARK
Odense
COPENHAGEN
GERMANY

THE BRITISH ISLES

LYING OFF THE COAST of mainland Europe, the British Isles consist of two main islands, Ireland and Great Britain, and many smaller islands. England, Scotland, Wales, and Northern Ireland form the United Kingdom (U.K.). The Republic of Ireland became independent of the U.K. in 1921.

UNITED KINGDOM
P 58 million
L English

NATURAL FEATURES
The highest point in the British Isles is Ben Nevis in Scotland at a height of 1,343 m (4,406 ft)

Shetland Is.

Orkney Is.

Aberdeen

NORTH SE

HIGHLANDS

GRAMPIAN MTS.

SCOTLAND

Edinburgh

Loch Ness

Firth

Loch Lomond

Glasgow

SOUTHERN UPL

Lewis

Skye

North Uist

South Uist

Barra

Coll

Tiree

Mull

Colonsay

Jura

Islay

Arran

Kintyre

Outer Hebrides

Londonderry

ATLANTIC OCEAN

N O R T H   S E A

UNITED KINGDOM

Isle of Man
(to U.K.)

I R I S H   S E A

Tees

PENNINES
LAKE
DISTRICT

Kingston
upon Hull

Leeds
Bradford
Manchester
Sheffield

Liverpool

Stoke-on-Trent
Derby
Nottingham
Leicester

Trent

Ouse

The
Fens

Wolverhampton
Birmingham
Coventry

E N G L A N D

CAMBRIAN MTS.

Anglesey

WALES

BRECON
BEACONS

Severn

Thames

LONDON

Cardiff

Bristol

EXMOOR

Southampton

Isle of Wight

DARTMOOR

Plymouth

E n g l i s h   C h a n n e l

Channel Is.

Guernsey (to U.K.)

Jersey
(to U.K.)

I R E L A N D

DUBLIN

Galway

Shannon

Shannon

Liffey

Barrow

Blackwater

Cork

Isles of
Scilly

N

200km
100miles

0   50   100

0   100   200

IRELAND
P 3.5 million
L Irish, English

CLIMATE
Warmed by the Gulf
Stream, the climate is mild
but changeable. Rainfall
is well distributed
throughout the year.

INDUSTRY
Pharmaceuticals, aerospace industry, oil, natural
gas, dairy products, computer parts, livestock.
Ireland has one of Europe's fastest growing economies.

SPAIN AND PORTUGAL

SUPREME SKILL IN shipbuilding and navigation enabled both Spain and Portugal to become the most powerful empires of the 16th century. Both have a seafaring history; Christopher Columbus sailed to America in 1492, and Vasco da Gama, the Portuguese explorer, was the first to sail around Africa to India in 1497.

INDUSTRY
Fishing, car manufacture, olives, cork, ship building, citrus fruit, tourism. Spain and Portugal are famous for fortified wines. Sherry is named after Jerez de la Frontera, Spain, and Port after Porto, Portugal.

CLIMATE
Spain's coastal areas are milder than the central plateau, which has a more extreme temperature range. Almeria, Spain, contains Europe's only desert. Portugal's Mediterranean climate is moderated by the Atlantic.

OCEAN

ATLANTIC

Oviedo

Santiago de Compostela

Galicia

Minho

Esla Res.

Porto

Douro

Coimbra

Tagus

Alcântara Res.

LISBON

Guadiana

Setúbal

Beja

SIERR

Lagos

Sevilla

Faro

PORTUGAL
P 9.9 million
L Portuguese

Gibralta
GIBRALTA
(to U.K.)

Strait o

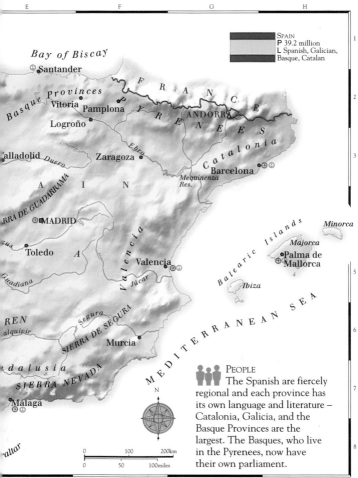

E   F   G   H

SPAIN
P 39.2 million
L Spanish, Galician, Basque, Catalan

Bay of Biscay
⊕ Santander

F R A N C E

Basque provinces
Vitoria • Pamplona
Logroño •

P Y R E N E E S

ANDORRA

Catalonia

alladolid *Duero*
Zaragoza •
Ebro

Barcelona • ⊕⊕

Mequinenza Res.

I N

RRA DE GUADARRAMA
⊕■ MADRID

us

Toledo •
A

Guadiana

Valencia

Valencia • ⊕⊕
Júcar

Balearic Islands

Minorca

Majorca
• Palma de
⊕ Mallorca

Ibiza

REN
alquivir
Segura
SIERRA DE SEGURA

Murcia •

M E D I T E R R A N E A N   S E A

dalusia
SIERRA NEVADA

• Málaga ⊕⊕

altar

N

0   100   200km
0   50   100miles

PEOPLE
The Spanish are fiercely regional and each province has its own language and literature – Catalonia, Galicia, and the Basque Provinces are the largest. The Basques, who live in the Pyrenees, now have their own parliament.

E   F   G   H

FRANCE

FOLLOWING THE FRENCH Revolution (1789–99), France became Europe's first modern republic, and possessed a colonial empire that included parts of Asia and Africa. France and Spain jointly governed Andorra from 1278. In 1993 the principality held its first full elections. The country of Monaco is a lucrative banking centre.

PEOPLE
Despite a strong national identity, the Bretons, Normans, Alsatians, Corsicans, and the Monegasque from Monaco still maintain their regional traditions.

ANDORRA
P 58,000
L Catalan

COMMUNICATIONS
The French lead the world in high-speed train technology. First run in 1981, the TGV (*Train à Grande Vitesse*) is one of the world's fastest trains, with a top speed of 300 km/h (186 mph).

N

0 75 150km
0 50 100miles

English Channel

Cherbourg
Le Havre
Channel Islands (to U.K.)
Caen
NORMANDY
Île d'Ouessant
Brest
BRITTANY
Rennes
Le Mans
Belle Île
Loire
Nantes
Poitie
ATLANTIC OCEAN
Bordeaux
Garonne
PYRENEE
SPAI

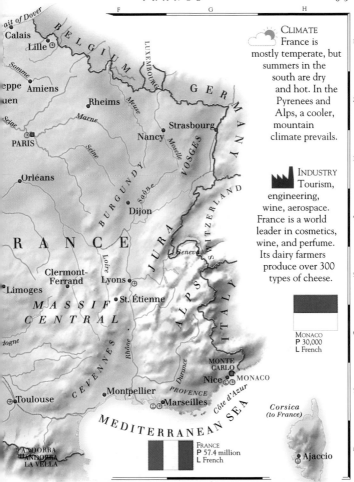

F   G   H

Strait of Dover

Calais

Lille

BELGIUM

LUXEMBOURG

GERMANY

Somme

eppe   Amiens

uen

Rheims

Marne

Strasbourg

Seine

Nancy

Meuse

Moselle

PARIS

Seine

VOSGES

Orléans

BURGUNDY

Saône

SWITZERLAND

Dijon

JURA

Loire

Geneva

F R A N C E

Clermont-
Ferrand

Lyons

ALPS

ITALY

Limoges

St. Étienne

M A S S I F

C E N T R A L

Rhône

dogne

C E V E N N E S

Durance

MONTE
CARLO

Nice   MONACO

Toulouse

Montpellier

PROVENCE

Marseilles

Côte d'Azur

M E D I T E R R A N E A N   S E A

ANDORRA
ANDORRA
LA VELLA

1

2

3

4

5

6

7

8

CLIMATE
France is
mostly temperate, but
summers in the
south are dry
and hot. In the
Pyrenees and
Alps, a cooler,
mountain
climate prevails.

INDUSTRY
Tourism,
engineering,
wine, aerospace.
France is a world
leader in cosmetics,
wine, and perfume.
Its dairy farmers
produce over 300
types of cheese.

MONACO
P 30,000
L French

Corsica
(to France)

Ajaccio

FRANCE
P 57.4 million
L French

THE LOW COUNTRIES

BELGIUM, THE NETHERLANDS, and
Luxembourg are known as the
"Low Countries"
because they are flat
and low-lying. Much of the
Netherlands lies below sea
level and has been
reclaimed from the sea.
The Low Countries, also
called "Benelux", are
Europe's most densely
populated countries.

CLIMATE
The region is mostly
temperate. Coastal areas
are mildest, warmed by
the Gulf Stream.
Luxembourg's
winters are cold
and snowy.

GERMANY

Groningen

Leeuwarden

Assen

West Frisian Is.

Waddenzee

IJsselmeer

Flevoland

IJssel Zwolle

Enschede

Apeldoorn

Arnhem

Rhine

Nijmegen

AMSTERDAM

Haarlem

Utrecht

's-Hertogenbosch

The Hague

Rotterdam

Dordrecht

Breda

NETHERLANDS

NORTH SEA

NETHERLANDS
P 15.3 million

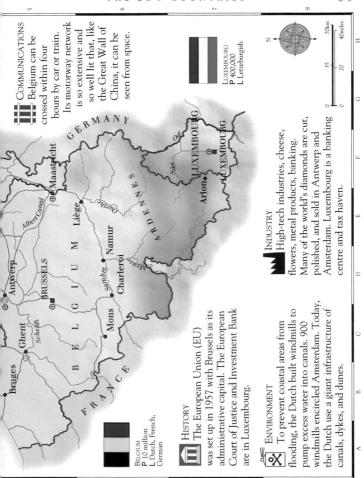

COMMUNICATIONS

Belgium can be crossed within four hours by car or train. Its motorway network is so extensive and so well lit that, like the Great Wall of China, it can be seen from space.

LUXEMBOURG
P 400,000
L Letzeburgish

GERMANY

Maastricht

ARDENNES

Liège

Albert Canal

Antwerp

Sambre

Namur

Charleroi

Meuse

Ourthe

Sûre

Our

LUXEMBOURG

LUXEMBOURG

Arlon

BRUSSELS

Ghent

Schelat

Mons

B   E   L   G   I   U   M

Bruges

F   R   A   N   C   E

N

70km

40miles

35

20

0

0

BELGIUM
P 10 million
L Dutch, French, German

HISTORY

The European Union (EU) was set up in 1957 with Brussels as its administrative capital. The European Court of Justice and Investment Bank are in Luxembourg.

INDUSTRY

High-tech industries, cheese, flowers, metal products, banking. Many of the world's diamonds are cut, polished, and sold in Antwerp and Amsterdam. Luxembourg is a banking centre and tax haven.

ENVIRONMENT

To prevent coastal areas from flooding, the Dutch built windmills to pump excess water into canals. 900 windmills encircled Amsterdam. Today, the Dutch use a giant infrastructure of canals, dykes, and dunes.

GERMANY

It was not until 1871 that many small independent states were united under Prussia to form Germany. After 1945, the country was divided again, into a democratic West Germany and a Soviet-dominated East Germany. Reunified in 1990, Germany is, with France, a leading member of the European Union and is currently Europe's strongest economic power.

INDUSTRY

Cars, heavy and precision engineering, electronics, chemicals. Germany has a strong industrial sector and is Europe's main car producer.

POLAND

BALTIC SEA

⊕ BERLIN • Potsdam

Rügen
Oder
Mecklenburg Bay
Rostock
L. Müritz
Magdeburg
Elb
SAXONY
Brunswick
Mittelland Canal
HARZ
DENMARK
Kiel Bay
Kiel
Lübeck
Schwerin
Hamburg
Bremen
Hanover
Weser
Bielefeld
Elbe

NORTH SEA
North Frisian
Helgoland Bay
East Frisian Is.
Dortmund-Ems Canal
Ems
Münster
Essen

NETHERLANDS

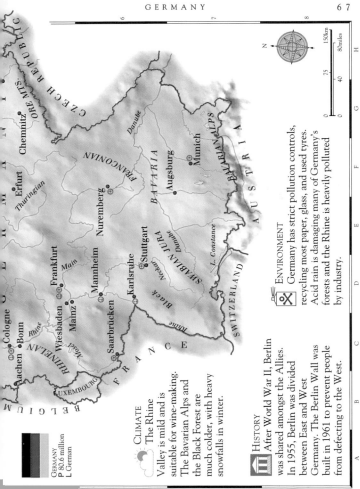

N

150km
80miles

0   40   75

CLIMATE
The Rhine Valley is mild and is suitable for wine-making. The Bavarian Alps and the Black Forest are much colder, with heavy snowfalls in winter.

HISTORY
After World War II, Berlin was shared amongst the Allies. In 1955, Berlin was divided between East and West Germany. The Berlin Wall was built in 1961 to prevent people from defecting to the West.

ENVIRONMENT
Germany has strict pollution controls, recycling most paper, glass, and used tyres. Acid rain is damaging many of Germany's forests and the Rhine is heavily polluted by industry.

GERMANY
P 80.6 million
L German

CZECH REPUBLIC

ORE MTS.

Chemnitz

Erfurt

Thuringian

FRANCONIAN

Danube

BAVARIA

Augsburg

Munich

BAVARIAN ALPS

Nuremberg

Cologne

Bonn

Aachen

RHINELAND

Rhine

Wiesbaden

Mainz

Moel

Saarbrücken

Frankfurt

Main

Mannheim

Karlsruhe

Neckar

Stuttgart

Black Forest

SWABIAN JURA

Danube

L. Constance

AUSTRIA

SWITZERLAND

Rhine

F R A N C E

B E L G I U M

LUXEMBOURG

A   B   C   D

SWITZERLAND AND AUSTRIA

ONCE THE CENTRE OF the vast Hapsburg Empire, Austria became an independent country in 1918. Switzerland has been a neutral country since 1815, and many international organizations, such as the Red Cross, have their headquarters there. Liechtenstein is closely allied to Switzerland, which handles its foreign relations.

LIECHTENSTEI
P 30,000
L German

SWITZERLAND
P 6.9 million
L German,
French, Italian

L. Constance
Winterthur
Bregenz
Basle
Rhine
St. Gallen
Zurich
L. Zurich
LIECHTENSTE
Aare
VADUZ
L. Biel
L. Lucerne
BERN
SWITZERLAND
L. Neuchâtel
L. Thun
A
L
P
S
Lausanne
Geneva
L. Genev
BERNESE ALPS
Rhône
Œneva
L. Maggiore
PENNINE ALPS
L. Lugano

N

0   50   100km
0   25   50miles

COMMUNICATIONS

The St. Gotthard road tunnel runs under the Swiss Alps. At over 16 km (10 miles) in length, it is the world's longest road tunnel.

A   B   C   D

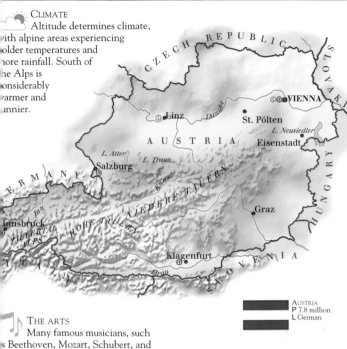

CLIMATE
Altitude determines climate, with alpine areas experiencing colder temperatures and more rainfall. South of the Alps is considerably warmer and sunnier.

AUSTRIA
P 7.8 million
L German

THE ARTS
Many famous musicians, such as Beethoven, Mozart, Schubert, and Brahms, lived and worked in Vienna.

NATURAL FEATURES
The Alps form part of an almost continuous mountain-belt, stretching from the Pyrenees in France to the Himalayas in Asia. They are also the source of Europe's largest rivers – the Rhine, Rhône, and Danube.

INDUSTRY
Pharmaceuticals, financial services, tourism, chemicals, electrical engineering. Liechtenstein is the centre of world dental manufacture. False teeth and dental materials are exported to over 100 countries.

CENTRAL EUROPE

HISTORICALLY AN
unstable part of the
continent, central
Europe became part
of the Eastern Bloc after World
War II. Czechoslovakia and
Poland had governments with
strong ties to the former U.S.S.R.
In 1989, they broke away from
communism, and in 1993
Czechoslovakia split into the
Czech Republic and Slovakia.
Poland is still moving
slowly towards a
market economy.

CZECH REPUBLIC
P 10.4 million
L Czech

CLIMATE

Central Europe has a
continental climate, with wet
springs, late summers, and cold
winters. Snow can cover eastern Poland
for almost three months of each year.

0   75   150km
0   50   100miles

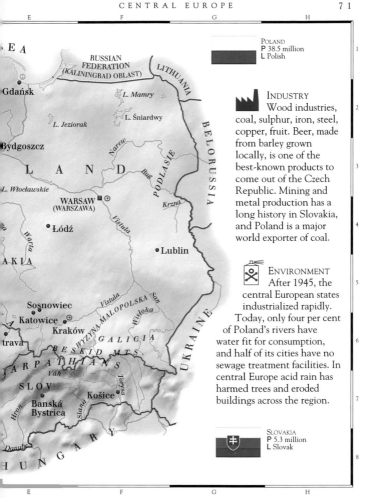

E F G H

POLAND
P 38.5 million
L Polish

INDUSTRY
Wood industries, coal, sulphur, iron, steel, copper, fruit. Beer, made from barley grown locally, is one of the best-known products to come out of the Czech Republic. Mining and metal production has a long history in Slovakia, and Poland is a major world exporter of coal.

ENVIRONMENT
After 1945, the central European states industrialized rapidly. Today, only four per cent of Poland's rivers have water fit for consumption, and half of its cities have no sewage treatment facilities. In central Europe acid rain has harmed trees and eroded buildings across the region.

SLOVAKIA
P 5.3 million
L Slovak

ITALY AND MALTA

THE BOOT-SHAPED PENINSULA of Italy stretches from the Alps to the Ionian Sea and includes Sardinia, Sicily, and other small, offshore islands. Italy also contains two independent enclaves – the Vatican City in Rome and the Republic of San Marino near Rimini. The Romans, Arabs, French, Turks, Spanish, and British have all fought for or colonized Malta, which has been independent since 1964.

PEOPLE

The Venetians were a seafaring people, whose ships carried silks and spices from Asia. The Venetian trader and explorer Marco Polo is said to have brought the recipe for pasta from China.

HISTORY

Italy was once a collection of small kingdoms and city-states, which were vulnerable to internal wars. It was united in 1870, through the efforts of the soldier Guiseppe Garibaldi and the politician Count Camillo di Cavour.

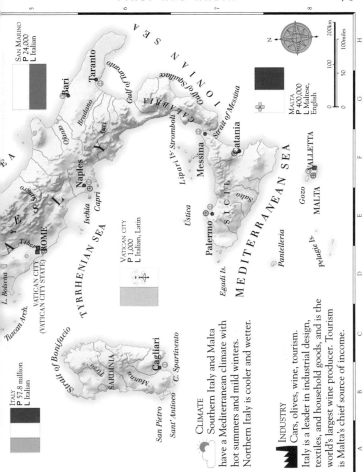

SAN MARINO
P 24,000
L Italian

MALTA,
P 400,000
L Maltese,
English

VATICAN CITY
P 1,000
L Italian, Latin

ITALY
P 57.8 million
L Italian

IONIAN SEA

Bari
Taranto

Gulf of Taranto

Bradano

Ofanto

Agri

CALABRIA

Gulf of Squillace

Strait of Messina

Messina

Lipari Is. *Stromboli*

Catania

SICILY

Salso

VALLETTA

Gozo

MALTA

Palermo

Ustica

MEDITERRANEAN SEA

Pantelleria

Pelagie Is.

Egadi Is.

Naples

Garano

Ischia

Capri

TYRRHENIAN SEA

ROME

Tiber

L. Bolsena

VATICAN CITY
(VATICAN CITY STATE)

Tuscan Arch.

ITALY

Strait of Bonifacio

Tirso

SARDINIA

Mannu

Cagliari

C. Spartivento

San Pietro

Sant'Antioco

CLIMATE
Southern Italy and Malta
have a Mediterranean climate with
hot summers and mild winters.
Northern Italy is cooler and wetter.

INDUSTRY
Cars, olives, wine, tourism.
Italy is a leader in industrial design,
textiles, and household goods, and is the
world's largest wine producer. Tourism
is Malta's chief source of income.

N

200km

100miles

100

50

SOUTH CENTRAL EUROPE

FOR CENTURIES the countries of this region have had strong ties with Europe. In the early 1990s Slovenia, Croatia, and Bosnia and Herzegovina declared their independence from Yugoslavia, to which they had been annexed after World War 1. This area boasts the snow-capped Alps, the sunny Adriatic Sea in the south, as well as Hungary's fertile plain.

SLOVENIA
P 2 million
L Slovene

CROATIA
P 4.9 million
L Croatian

CLIMATE
The climate in the region is just as varied as its geography. The interior has a continental climate, with warm summers and bitterly cold winters. Coastal areas in Croatia benefit from Mediterranean temperatures suitable for growing plums, apricots, and grapes.

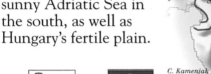

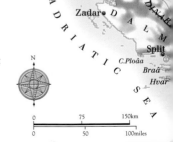

A U S T R I A

Za

Maribor

Čakove

LJUBLJANA

Sava

ZAGREB

SLOVENIA

C R

Kupa

Krerm

C. Kamenjak

Prijedo

Cres

Una

Pag

D A L M

Zadar

D I N A R

A D R I A T I C   S E A

Split

C.Ploča

Braå

Hvar

N

0   75   150km

0   50   100miles

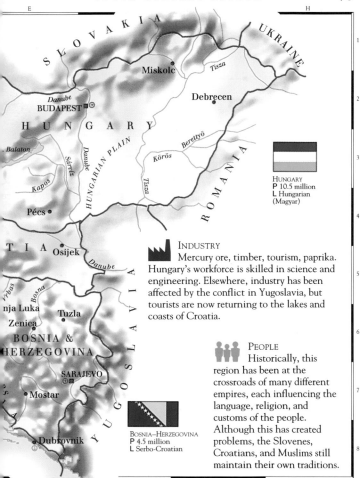

HUNGARY
P 10.5 million
L Hungarian
(Magyar)

INDUSTRY
Mercury ore, timber, tourism, paprika. Hungary's workforce is skilled in science and engineering. Elsewhere, industry has been affected by the conflict in Yugoslavia, but tourists are now returning to the lakes and coasts of Croatia.

PEOPLE
Historically, this region has been at the crossroads of many different empires, each influencing the language, religion, and customs of the people. Although this has created problems, the Slovenes, Croatians, and Muslims still maintain their own traditions.

BOSNIA–HERZEGOVINA
P 4.5 million
L Serbo-Croatian

SOUTHEAST EUROPE

THIS REGION IS often referred to as the Balkans, from the Turkish word for "mountain". It is made up of countries that have a long history of invasion and occupation. From its source in the Alps, the mighty River Danube flows eastwards through Romania and Bulgaria, before pouring into the Black Sea.

YUGOSLAVIA
P 10.6 million
L Serbo-Croatian

ROMANIA
P 23.4 million
L Romanian

BLACK SEA

TURKEY

Dobrich

Varna

Shumen

Burgas

B U L G A R I A

Pleven
Sliven

Tundzha

BALKAN MTS

Stara Zagora

Plovdiv

Maritsa

RHODOPE MTS

Struma

SOFIA
(SOFIYA)

BALKAN MTS

Iskâr

Niš

Leskovac

KOPAONIK

Kosovska
Mitrovica

Peć

Priština

Prizren

Kumanovo

SKOPJE

Vardar

MACEDONIA

Gostivar

Bitola

G R E E C E

L. Prespa

L. Ohrid

NORTH ALBANIAN ALPS

Montenegro

Podgorica

*Drin
Gulf*

TIRANE
(TIRANA)

A L B A N I A

Vlorë

Vijosë

A D R I A T I C   S E A

BOS

BULGARIA
P 8.9 million
L Bulgarian

MACEDONIA
P 1.9 million
L Macedonian

ALBANIA
P 3.3 million
L Albania

HISTORY

Over the past decade all the countries in this region have gained independence from the former Russian communist bloc. This led to the breakup of the former Yugoslavia in 1991. When the states of Serbia and Montenegro combined to form the new Federal Republic of Yugoslavia, it resulted in a war which lasted from 1991–95.

INDUSTRY

Coal, wine, tobacco, iron ore, tourism. Black Sea tourism is being developed in Romania to generate income to help improve the lives of the people. In the foothills of the Balkan Mountains in Bulgaria most of the world's rose oil is produced.

CLIMATE

Hot or cold winds from Russia can bring spells of extreme weather in Romania and Bulgaria. Snow may even stay on the peaks until mid-summer. Yugoslavia and Macedonia have warm summers that are good for growing early fruit crops.

N

0   125   250km

0   75   150miles

GREECE

SURROUNDED BY THE Aegean, Ionian, and Cretan seas, no part of Greece is more than 137 km (85 miles) from the coast. Its territory includes the mainland on the Balkan peninsula, and more than 1,400 islands. The country is mountainous and less than one-third of the land is cultivated. Greece gained its independence in 1830 after a long and fierce war, ending 400 years of Turkish rule.

CLIMATE

Northwestern Greece is alpine, while parts of Crete are almost subtropical. The islands and the large central plain of the mainland have a Mediterranean climate, with high summer temperatures and mild winters.

ENVIRONMENT

Athens suffers from smog, known as *nefos*, which damages its ancient monuments. The Parthenon, part of the Acropolis, has suffered more erosion in the previous two decades than in the past two thousand years.

GREECE
P 10.2 million
L Greek

HISTORY

Regarded as the founders of democracy, the ancient Greeks were advanced for their time. They were the first to study medicine, geometry, and physics (on a scientific basis), and Greece was home to great thinkers such as Plato, Aristotle, and Socrates.

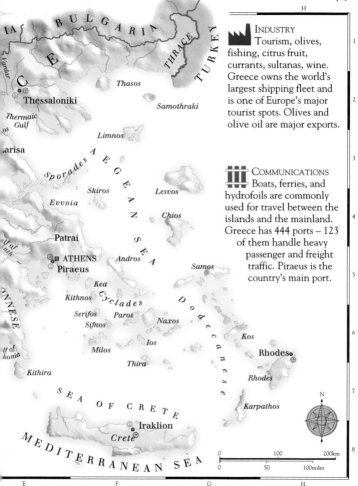

INDUSTRY
Tourism, olives, fishing, citrus fruit, currants, sultanas, wine. Greece owns the world's largest shipping fleet and is one of Europe's major tourist spots. Olives and olive oil are major exports.

COMMUNICATIONS
Boats, ferries, and hydrofoils are commonly used for travel between the islands and the mainland. Greece has 444 ports – 123 of them handle heavy passenger and freight traffic. Piraeus is the country's main port.

THE BALTIC STATES AND BELORUSSIA

LITHUANIA, ESTONIA, AND LATVIA – the three Baltic States – were the first republics to declare independence from the Soviet Union in 1990–91. There is now tension between native Estonians and Russians, who make up a third of the population. Belorussia's capital, Minsk, is the headquarters of the organization that brings together former Soviet States – the Confederation of Independent States (CIS).

PEOPLE
Russians, Belorussians, and Ukrainians resettled in Latvia when it was part of the U.S.S.R. Today Latvians make up only about half of the whole population, and they are a minority in the capital.

ESTONIA
P 1.6 million
L Estonian

LATVIA
P 2.7 million
L Latvian

BELORUSSIA
P 10.3 million
L Belorussian

LITHUANIA
P 3.8 million
L Lithuanian

RUSSIA

Gulf of Finland

ESTONIA

⊕ TALLINN

Narva

Emajõgi

L. Peipus

Tartu

Võrtsjärv

Hiiumaa

Saaremaa

Gulf of Riga

⊕ RIGA

L A T

Venta

B A L T I C

S E A

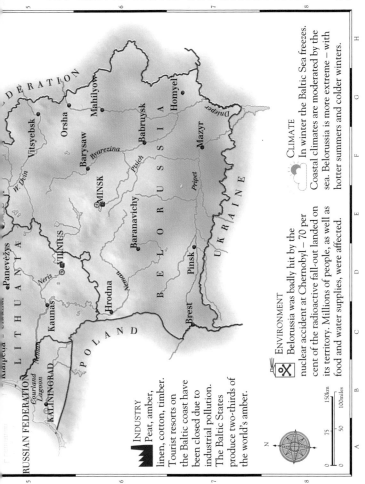

INDUSTRY
Peat, amber, linen, cotton, timber. Tourist resorts on the Baltic coast have been closed due to industrial pollution. The Baltic States produce two-thirds of the world's amber.

ENVIRONMENT
Belorussia was badly hit by the nuclear accident at Chernobyl – 70 per cent of the radioactive fall-out landed on its territory. Millions of people, as well as food and water supplies, were affected.

CLIMATE
In winter the Baltic Sea freezes. Coastal climates are moderated by the sea. Belorussia is more extreme – with hotter summers and colder winters.

RUSSIAN FEDERATION

Courland Lagoon

KALININGRAD

Kaunas

Panevėžys

LITHUANIA

Klaipeda

VILNIUS

Neris

Hrodna

Nemunas

POLAND

Brest

Pinsk

Baranavichy

MINSK

Baryshaw

Byarezina

Pripet

Mazyr

Babruysk

Orsha

Mahilyow

Homyel

Vitsyebsk

W. Dvina

BELORUSSIA

UKRAINE

Dnyapro

Pripch

DERATION

0   75   150km
0   50   100miles

N

EUROPEAN RUSSIA

SPANNING THE TWO continents of Europe and Asia, the Russian Federation is the world's largest country. In 1917, the world's first communist government took power and in 1923, Russia became the U.S.S.R., which included many territories that were once part of the Russian Empire. Economic reforms in the 1980s led to changes resulting in the fall of communism in 1991.

INDUSTRY
Oil, gas, gold, diamonds, hydrocarbons, precious metals. Russia has large reserves of iron, coal, and nickel. Huge factories, which have grown without environmental controls, are causing pollution problems.

Novaya Zemlya

KARA SEA

Kara Vrgach I.

Kara Strait

Vorkuta

Usa

BARENTS SEA

Pechora

Kolguyev I.

Murmansk

L. Imandra

KOLA

L. Pyaozero PENINSULA

L. Topozero

WHITE SEA

Arkhangel'sk

FINLAND

L. Segozero

Onega

L. Ladoga

L. Onega

RUSSIAN

ESTONIA

St. Petersburg

LATVIA

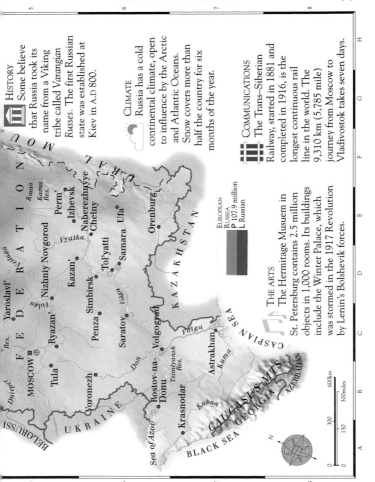

HISTORY

Some believe that Russia took its name from a Viking tribe called *Varangian Russes*. The first Russian state was established at Kiev in A.D 800.

CLIMATE

Russia has a cold continental climate, open to influence by the Arctic and Atlantic Oceans. Snow covers more than half the country for six months of the year.

COMMUNICATIONS

The Trans–Siberian Railway, started in 1881 and completed in 1916, is the longest continuous rail line in the world. The 9,310 km (5,785 mile) journey from Moscow to Vladivostok takes seven days.

EUROPEAN
RUSSIA
P 107.9 million
L Russian

THE ARTS

The Hermitage Musuem in St. Petersburg contains 2.5 million objects in 1,000 rooms. Its buildings include the Winter Palace, which was stormed in the 1917 Revolution by Lenin's Bolshevik forces.

0   300   600km
0   150   300miles

Ukraine and the Caucasus

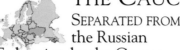

Separated from the Russian Federation by the Caucasus mountains, the newly independent Caucasian Republics – Armenia, Azerbaijan, and Georgia – are rich in natural resources. The Ukraine, Europe's largest country, is dominated by a flat and fertile plain.

Environment
As a result of the 1986 Chernobyl nuclear disaster, 4 million Ukrainians live in radioactive areas. In 1994, reactors from the Chernobyl plant were still being used to provide nuclear power.

MOLDAVIA
P 4.4 million
L Romanian

Climate
Ukraine and Moldavia have a continental climate, with distinctive seasons. Armenia, Azerbaijan, and Georgia are protected from cold air from the north by the Caucasus mountains.

N

| 0 | 150 | 300km |
| 0 | 75 | 150miles |

Industry
Coal, iron, cars, wine, citrus fruit, cotton, minerals. The Ukraine was known as the "breadbasket" of the Soviet Union as its steppes were extensively cultivated. Georgia's known oil reserves are as yet unexploited.

BELORUSSIA
POLAND
Luts'k
Rivne
L'viv
Chernihiv
Chernobyl'
Kiev Res.
KIEV
Zhytomyr
Ternopil'
Khmel'nyts'kyy
Bila Tserkva
Vinnytsya
SLOVAKIA
Ivano-Frankivs'k
Dniester
UKRA
HUNGARY
Chernivtsi
MOLDAVIA
ROMANIA
CHISINAU
Mykolayiv
Odesa
Sluch
Styr

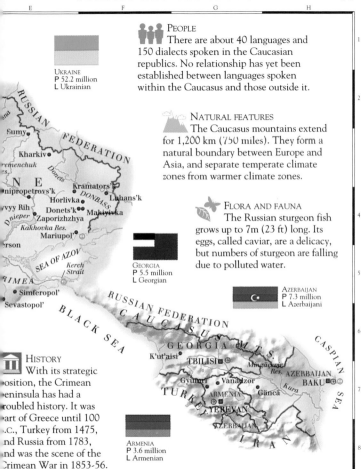

PEOPLE

There are about 40 languages and 150 dialects spoken in the Caucasian republics. No relationship has yet been established between languages spoken within the Caucasus and those outside it.

NATURAL FEATURES

The Caucasus mountains extend for 1,200 km (750 miles). They form a natural boundary between Europe and Asia, and separate temperate climate zones from warmer climate zones.

FLORA AND FAUNA

The Russian sturgeon fish grows up to 7m (23 ft) long. Its eggs, called caviar, are a delicacy, but numbers of sturgeon are falling due to polluted water.

UKRAINE
P 52.2 million
L Ukrainian

GEORGIA
P 5.5 million
L Georgian

AZERBAIJAN
P 7.3 million
L Azerbaijani

ARMENIA
P 3.6 million
L Armenian

HISTORY

With its strategic position, the Crimean peninsula has had a troubled history. It was part of Greece until 100 B.C., Turkey from 1475, and Russia from 1783, and was the scene of the Crimean War in 1853-56.

Sumy
Kharkiv
Kremenchuk Res.
Dnipropetrovs'k
Kryvyy Rih
Kherson
Kramators'k
Horlivka
Donets'k
Zaporizhzhya
Makiyivka
Kakhovka Res.
Mariupol'
DONBASS
Donets
Luhans'k
RUSSIAN FEDERATION
DESNA

SEA OF AZOV
Kerch Strait
CRIMEA
Simferopol'
Sevastopol'

BLACK SEA

RUSSIAN FEDERATION
CAUCASUS
GEORGIA MTS.
K'ut'aisi
TBILISI
Mingäçevir Res.
Gyumri
Vanadzor
ARMENIA
YEREVAN
AZERBAIJAN
BAKU
Gäncä
Kura
AZERBAIJAN
CASPIAN SEA
TURKEY
IRAN

AFRICA

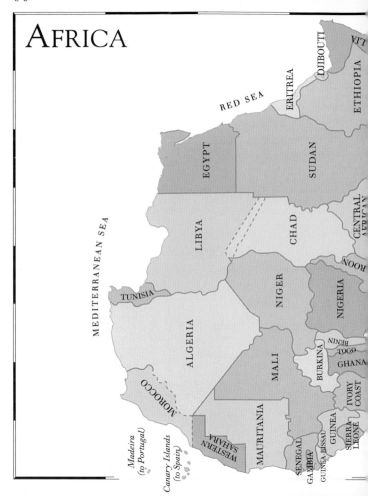

MEDITERRANEAN SEA

RED SEA

Madeira
(to Portugal)

Canary Islands
(to Spain)

MOROCCO

TUNISIA

ALGERIA

LIBYA

EGYPT

WESTERN SAHARA

MAURITANIA

MALI

NIGER

CHAD

SUDAN

ERITREA

DJIBOUTI

ETHIOPIA

VII

CENTRAL AFRICAN

ROON

NIGERIA

BENIN

TOGO

GHANA

BURKINA

IVORY COAST

GUINEA

SIERRA LEONE

GUINEA-BISSAU

GAMBIA

SENEGAL

SEYCHELLES

COMOROS

MADAGASCAR

KENYA

BURUNDI

TANZANIA

RWANDA

MALAWI

MOZAMBIQUE

ZIMBABWE

SWAZILAND

CONGO
(ZAIRE)

ZAMBIA

LESOTHO

ANGOLA

BOTSWANA

SOUTH
AFRICA

CONGO

NAMIBIA

GABON

SAO TOME & PRINCIPE

ATLANTIC OCEAN

AFRICA

Both tropics and the equator
run through Africa, the
warmest of all the continents.
The land around the tropics
is starved of rain creating great
deserts such as the Sahara
and the Kalahari. In contrast,
high rainfall around the
equator has produced lush
tropical rainforests.

NORTHWEST AFRICA

SPANNING THE continent of Africa, from the Atlantic to the Red Sea, the Sahara covers 9 million sq km (3.5 million sq miles) and is the world's largest desert. Droughts and the over-use of land for farming are causing the Sahara to spread into the Sahel (semi-arid grasslands). Italy, the U.K., Spain, and France have all had colonies in this region.

Strait of Gibraltar

Ceuta (to Spain)   Melilla (to Spain)

Tangier

RABAT
Casablanca

Fez

MOROCCO
Marrakesh

Agadir

ATLAS MTS

Béch

ATLANTIC OCEAN

EL AAIUN

Dakhla

WESTERN SAHARA

MAURITANIA

A   I

M

Morocco occupied the whole of Western Sahara in 1979.

INDUSTRY
Oil, gas, phosphates, tourism, olives, dates, fruit. Morocco and Tunisia attract millions of tourists every year. They are also leading phosphate producers. Algeria and Libya have significant oil reserves.

MOROCCO
P 27 million
L Arabic

CLIMATE
Coastal areas have a temperate climate with hot, dry summers and wet winters. Mountain areas are cooler. Most areas are affected by the many different kinds of Sahara wind, such as the *sirocco*, the *chergui*, and the *chili*.

NATURAL FEATURES
The Atlas Mountains extend over 2,410 km (1,500 miles) from the Canary Islands in the Atlantic to Tunisia. Like the Alps, the Atlas Mountains were formed when the continental plates of Europe and Africa pushed together.

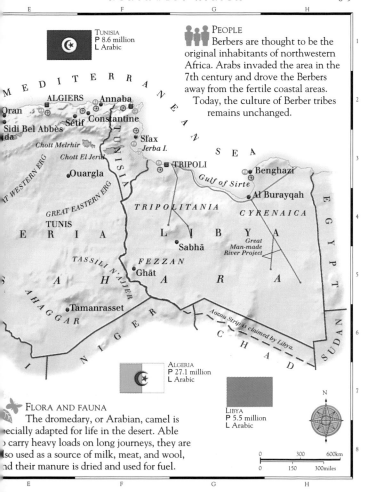

TUNISIA
P 8.6 million
L Arabic

PEOPLE
Berbers are thought to be the original inhabitants of northwestern Africa. Arabs invaded the area in the 7th century and drove the Berbers away from the fertile coastal areas. Today, the culture of Berber tribes remains unchanged.

M E D I T E R R A N E A N

S E A

ALGIERS Annaba

Oran

Sidi Bel Abbès Sétif Constantine

da

Chott Melrhir

Sfax

Jerba I.

Chott El Jerid

T WESTERN ERG

Ouargla

GREAT EASTERN ERG

TUNIS

E R I A

TASSILI N'AJJER

A

AHAGGAR

Tamanrasset

HAGGAR

TRIPOLI

Gulf of Sirte

Benghazi

Al Burayqah

T R I P O L I T A N I A

C Y R E N A I C A

L I B Y A

Sabhā

Great Man-made River Project

F E Z Z A N

Ghāt

A

R

A

N I G E R

C

Aozou Strip is claimed by Libya.

E G Y P T

S U D A N

H A D

ALGERIA
P 27.1 million
L Arabic

LIBYA
P 5.5 million
L Arabic

N

0   300   600km
0   150   300miles

FLORA AND FAUNA
The dromedary, or Arabian, camel is specially adapted for life in the desert. Able to carry heavy loads on long journeys, they are also used as a source of milk, meat, and wool, and their manure is dried and used for fuel.

NORTHEAST AFRICA

THE NILE, THE LONGEST river in the world, carries rich mud from the highlands of Sudan into Egypt, creating some of the most fertile land in the world. About 99 per cent of Egypt's population live on the river's banks. Ethiopia, Somalia, and Sudan have been beset by drought, famine, and war and about half of Africa's 4.5 million refugees come from this area.

EGYPT
P 56.1 million
L Arabic

HISTORY

Hieroglyphs were a set of mysterious symbols until the discovery of the Rosetta Stone in 1799. The Stone is inscribed in three different scripts: ancient Greek, demotic, and hieroglyphs. By comparing the royal names in the scripts, hieroglyphs were finally deciphered 25 years later.

ERITREA
P 3.5 million
L Tigrinya,
Arabic

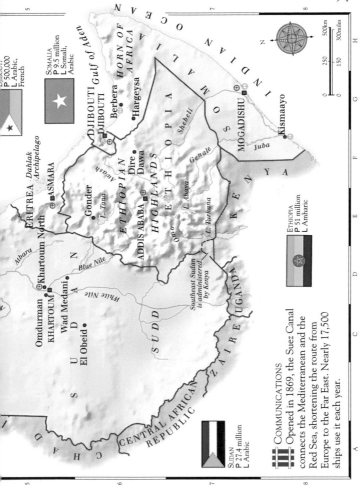

P 500,000
L Arabic,
French

SOMALIA
P 9.5 million
L Somali,
Arabic

INDIAN OCEAN

N

500km
300miles
0   250
0   150

Gulf of Aden

DJIBOUTI
DJIBOUTI   Berbera
            Hargeysa

HORN OF
AFRICA

SOMALIA

Dahlak
Archipelago

ERITREA

ASMARA

Awash

Shebeli

ETHIOPIAN

Dire
Dawa

Genale

Gonder

L. Tana

HIGHLANDS

MOGADISHU

Juba

Kismaayo

ADDIS ABABA

Omo

ETHIOPIA

L. Abaya

KENYA

L. Turkana

Khartoum North

ETHIOPIA
P 51 million
L Amharic

Atbara

Blue Nile

SUDAN

Omdurman
KHARTOUM

Wad Medani

El Obeid

White Nile

Southeast Sudan
is administered
by Kenya

UGANDA

ZAIRE

CENTRAL AFRICAN
REPUBLIC

CHAD

SUDAN
P 27.4 million
L Arabic

COMMUNICATIONS
Opened in 1869, the Suez Canal
connects the Mediterranean and the
Red Sea, shortening the route from
Europe to the Far East. Nearly 17,500
ships use it each year.

WEST AFRICA

BY 1914, MANY European countries, such as France, Britain, and Portugal, had divided up most of Africa between them. Despite independence, foreign companies still own many of the coffee and cocoa plantations in the region.

GAMBIA
P 900,000
L English

INDUSTRY
Bauxite, oil, gypsum, cocoa, phosphates, peanuts, fishing. This region produces nearly half of the world's supply of cocoa beans. The world's largest deposits of gypsum are found in Mauritania.

CLIMATE
Coastal areas have a tropical climate, with high temperatures and one or two rainy seasons. The hot and dry Sahel is marked by the dusty *harmattan* wind.

GUINEA
P 6.3 million
L French

GUINEA-BISSAU
P 1 million
L Portuguese

SIERRA LEONE
P 4.5 million
L English

WESTERN SAHARA

C. Blanc
C. Timiris

MAURITANIA

NOUAKCHOTT

L. Rkiz

Senegal

SENEGAL

DAKAR

BANJUL
GAMBIA

BAMAKO

BISSAU
GUINEA-BISSAU
Bijagós
Archipelago

GUINEA

Niger

CONAKRY

MONT DU TOURA

FREETOWN
SIERRA
LEONE

de Kosso

MONROVIA

YAMOUSSOUKE

ATLANTIC OCEAN

LIBERIA

IC

Ivor

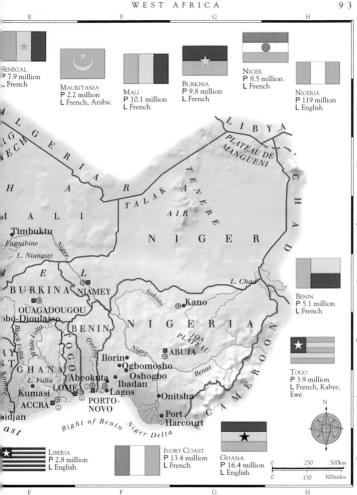

SENEGAL
P 7.9 million
L French

MAURITANIA
P 2.2 million
L French, Arabic

MALI
P 10.1 million
L French

BURKINA
P 9.8 million
L French

NIGER
P 8.5 million
L French

NIGERIA
P 119 million
L English

BENIN
P 5.1 million
L French

TOGO
P 3.9 million
L French, Kabye,
Ewe

LIBERIA
P 2.8 million
L English

IVORY COAST
P 13.4 million
L French

GHANA
P 16.4 million
L English

Timbuktu
Faguibine
L. Niangay
BURKINA
OUAGADOUGOU
bo-Dioulasso
BENIN
GHANA
L. Volta
Kumasi
ACCRA
idjan
NIAMEY
Kano
NIGERIA
ABUJA
Ilorin
Ogbomosho
Oshogbo
Ibadan
Onitsha
Port
Harcourt
LOME
PORTO-
NOVO
Abeokuta
Lagos
Bight of Benin
Niger Delta

ALGERIA
LIBYA
PLATEAU DE
MANGUENI
TALAK
TENERE
AIR
NIGER
L. Chad
Sokoto
JOS
PLATEAU
Niger
Benue
CAMEROON
CHAD

N

0   250   500km
0   150   300miles

CENTRAL AFRICA

MUCH OF THIS region is covered in dense tropical rainforest, drained by the Congo (Zaire) River, which forms a huge arc on its way to the Atlantic. In the 16th century Portugal and Spain set up trading posts on the west coast as part of the slave trade. Millions of Africans from this region were sent as slaves to the New World. Many people in coastal areas still speak Spanish and Portuguese.

CHAD
P 6 million
L French

INDUSTRY
Timber, oil, iron, cocoa, coffee, copper. Bélinga, Gabon, contains the world's largest iron ore deposits. Many central African countries have unexploited oil and gas reserves.

CENTRAL AFRICAN REPUBLIC
P 3.3 million
L French

CAMEROON
P 12.5 million
L French, English

EQUATORIAL GUINEA
P 400,000
L Spanish

LIBYA

Aozou Strip, claimed by Libya

TIBESTI

CHAD

NIGER

NIGERIA

L. Chad
Kousséri N'DJAMENA
Maroua
Garoua
Moundou Sarh
Chari
Logone
Erguig
Salamat

SUDAN

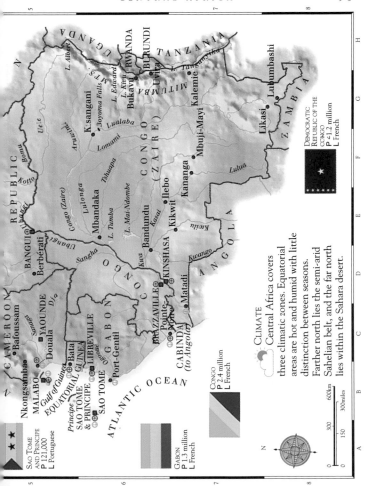

CAMEROON
Bafoussam
YAOUNDE
Douala
Sanaga
Dja
REPUBLIC
Bomu
Kotto
Uele
BANGUI
Berbérati
Ubangi
Congo (Zaire)
Sangha

Nkongsamba
MALABO
Gulf of Guinea
EQUATORIAL GUINEA
Bata
SAO TOME
LIBREVILLE
Principe
SAO TOME & PRINCIPE
Port-Gentil
GABON
Ogooué
ATLANTIC OCEAN

BRAZZAVILLE
Pointe-Noire
CONGO
Kouilou
CABINDA
(to Angola)
KINSHASA
Matadi

SUDAN
UGANDA
L. Albert
L. Edward
RWANDA
BURUNDI
TANZANIA
L. Kivu
Bukavu
Uvira
MITUMBA MTS.
L. Tanganyika
Kalemie
Lubumbashi
Likasi
ZAMBIA

K.sangani
Boyoma Falls
Aruwimi
Lualaba
Lomami
Tshuapa
Lulonga
CONGO (ZAIRE)
Mbandaka
L. Tumba
Kasai
Kwa
Bandundu
L. Mai-Ndombe
Ilebo
Kananga
Mbuji-Mayi
Lulua
Kikwit
Kwilu
Kasai
Kwango
ANGOLA

DEMOCRATIC REPUBLIC OF THE CONGO
P <1.2 million
L French

SAO TOME AND PRINCIPE
P 121,000
L Portuguese

CONGO
P 2.4 million
L French

GABON
P 1.3 million
L French

CLIMATE
Central Africa covers three climatic zones. Equatorial areas are hot and humid with little distinction between seasons. Farther north lies the semi-arid Sahelian belt, and the far north lies within the Sahara desert.

N

0 300 600km
0 150 300miles

CENTRAL EAST AFRICA

LARGE AREAS OF savannah, or grassland, in central Africa provide grazing for both domestic and wild animals. Industry is poorly developed in the region – Zambia, Rwanda, Burundi, and Uganda suffer from having no sea ports. Lake Victoria is the largest lake in Africa, and a source of the River Nile.

FLORA AND FAUNA

Poaching remains a major problem in this area. To combat this, all the countries in this region have set up wildlife parks to protect animals such as elephants and zebra.

INDUSTRY

Tobacco, coffee, tea, tourism, cloves, copper. Zambia is the world's fifth-largest producer of copper. Wildlife parks in this region attract thousands of tourists.

UGANDA
P 19.2 million
L English

RWANDA
P 7.5 million
L French,
Kinyarwanda

KENYA
P 26.1 million
L Swahili

SOMALIA

ETHIOPIA

SUDAN

Southeast Sudan
is administered
by Kenya

CHALBI
DESERT

KENYA

NAIROBI

ABERDARE
RANGE

Tana

Galana

OCEAN

Mombasa

Rift Valley

L. Turkana

Albert Nile

Victoria
Nile

L. Albert

L. Edward

L. Kyoga

UGANDA

KAMPALA

Lake
Victoria

Mwanza

L. Eyasi

L. Manyara

RUWENZORI

RWANDA

KIGALI

BUJUMBURA

BURUNDI

ZAIRE

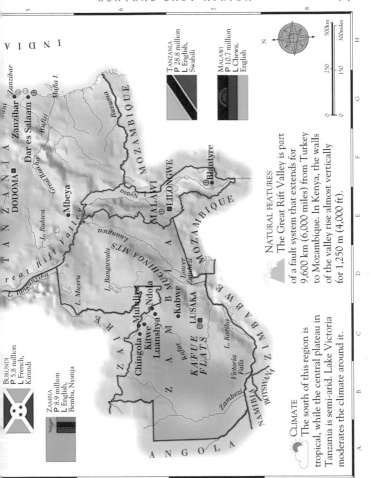

INDIA

Zanzibar
Zanzibar
Mafia I.

TANZANIA
Dar es Salaam
DODOMA
Mbeya
Rufiji
Great Ruaha
Ruvuma

MOZAMBIQUE

TANZANIA
P 28.8 million
L English,
Swahili

MALAWI
P 10.7 million
L Chewa,
English

NATURAL FEATURES
The Great Rift Valley is part of a fault system that extends for 9,600 km (6,000 miles) from Turkey to Mozambique. In Kenya, the walls of the valley rise almost vertically for 1,250 m (4,000 ft).

LILONGWE
MALAWI
Blantyre
L. Nyasa

Great Rift Valley
L. Rukwa
L. Tanganyika

MUCHINGA MTS.
L. Bangweulu
L. Mweru
Luangwa

ZAMBIA
Mufulira
Chingola
Kitwe
Ndola
Luanshya
Kabwe
LUSAKA
Kafue
L. Kariba
Zambezi
Lower Zambezi

KAFUE FLATS
Victoria Falls

BURUNDI
P 5.8 million
L French,
Kirundi

ZAMBIA
P 8.9 million
L English,
Bemba, Nyanja

CLIMATE
The south of this region is tropical, while the central plateau in Tanzania is semi-arid. Lake Victoria moderates the climate around it.

ZIMBABWE
MOZAMBIQUE
BOTSWANA
NAMIBIA
ANGOLA

N

500km
300miles
0 250
0 150

SOUTHERN AFRICA

SOUTHERN AFRICA'S RICH mineral resources, such as gold and diamonds, provide most of the wealth in this region, but South Africa dominates politics, work, and trade. All eight countries are independent, multi-racial democracies. South Africa had its first free elections in 1994 when Nelson Mandela was voted the country's first black president. Namibia won independence in 1990, but Angola is still torn apart by civil war.

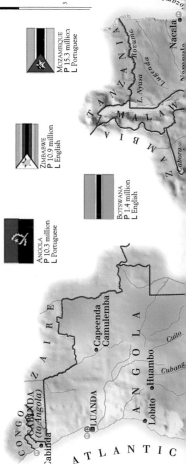

ANGOLA
P 10.3 million
L Portuguese

ZIMBABWE
P 10.9 million
L English

MOZAMBIQUE
P 15.3 million
L Portuguese

BOTSWANA
P 1.4 million
L English

CONGO

ZAIRE

CABINDA
(to Angola)

Cabinda

⊕ LUANDA

Capeenda Camulemba

A N G O L A

Lobito ● ● Huambo

Cuito

Cubang

ATLANTIC

TANZANIA

ZAMBIA

MALAWI

L. Nyasa

Luangwa

Cabora

Lugenda

Rovuma

Nacala

Mozambique Channel

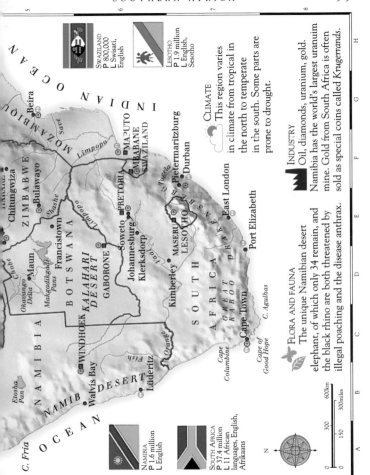

SWAZILAND
P 800,000
L Swsiati,
English

LESOTHO
P 1.9 million
L English,
Sesotho

INDIAN OCEAN

C. Fria

Beira

MOZAMBIQUE

Save

ZIMBABWE

Chitungwiza

Bulawayo

Limpopo

MAPUTO

MBABANE
SWAZILAND

Chobe

Shashe

Tugela

Pietermaritzburg

Durban

Maun

Francistown

Makgadikgadi
Pans

BOTSWANA

KALAHARI
DESERT

GABORONE

Soweto PRETORIA

Johannesburg

Klerksdorp

Vaal

Kimberley

MASERU

LESOTHO

East London

Okavango
Delta

NAMIBIA

WINDHOEK

S O U T H

A F R I C A

G R E A T

K A R O O

D R A K E N S B E R G

Port Elizabeth

Etosha
Pan

NAMIB

DESERT

Walvis Bay

Lüderitz

Orange

Fish

Cape
Columbine

Cape of
Good Hope

Cape Town

C. Agulhas

OCEAN

CLIMATE

This region varies in climate from tropical in the north to temperate in the south. Some parts are prone to drought.

INDUSTRY

Oil, diamonds, uranium, gold. Namibia has the world's largest uranuim mine. Gold from South Africa is often sold as special coins called *Krugerrands*.

FLORA AND FAUNA

The unique Namibian desert elephant, of which only 34 remain, and the black rhino are both threatened by illegal poaching and the disease anthrax.

NAMIBIA
P 1.6 million
L English

SOUTH AFRICA
P 37.4 million
L 11 African
languages, English,
Afrikaans

N

0   150   300
0   300   600km
     300miles

INDIAN OCEAN

THE SMALLEST of the world's oceans, the Indian Ocean has some 5,000 islands scattered across its area. Beneath its surface, three great mountain ranges converge towards the ocean's centre – an area of strong seismic and volcanic activity. The ocean's greatest depth, 7,440 m (24,400 ft), is in the Java Trench.

FLORA AND FAUNA

Owing to its position off the African coast, Madagascar is home to many unique animals, such as tenrecs, lemurs, and fossas.

ENVIRONMENT

The Indian Ocean is at risk from oil pollution from tankers carrying oil from the Persian Gulf.

CLIMATE

The monsoon winds blow over the Indian Ocean – from the southwest or from the northeast according to the season. The southwesterly monsoon brings heavy rains to southern Asia.

Port Said
Suez
Suez Canal
Nile
Kuwait
The Gulf
ARABIA
Djibouti
Aden
Gulf of Aden
RED SEA
Somali
C. Xaafuun
Socotra (to Yemen)
Ra's al Hadd
ARABIAN SEA
Karachi
Indus
Bombay
Lakshadweep Is. (to India)
MALDIVES
Madras
Cochin
A S I A
Ganges
Calcutta
Sri Lanka
Bay of Bengal
Andaman Is. (to India)
Nicobar Is. (to India)
ANDAMAN SEA
Irrawaddy
Mekong
Rangoon
Gulf of Thailand
SOUTH CHINA

MALDIVES
P 13.3 million
L Divehi

SEYCHELLES
P 69,000
L Creole,

COMOROS
P 497,000
L Arabic, French

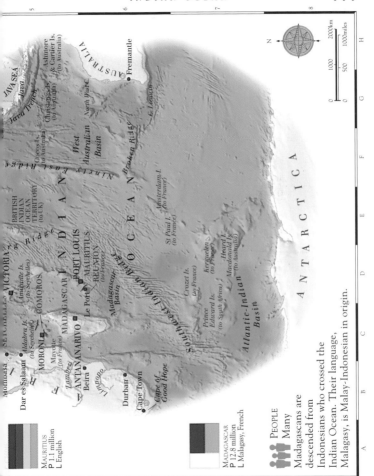

INDIAN OCEAN

ANTARCTICA

JAVA SEA
Java
Java Trench

AUSTRALIA
Fremantle

Ashmore & Cartier Is. (to Australia)
Christmas Is. (to Australia)
Cocos Is. (to Australia)
North West C.
C. Leeuwin

Broken Ridge

West Australian Basin

Ninety East Ridge

Amsterdam I. (to France)
St Paul I. (to France)

Kerguelen (to France)
Heard I. McDonald Is. (to Australia)

Crozet Is. (to France)
Prince Edward Is. (to South Africa)

BRITISH INDIAN OCEAN TERRITORY (to UK)

SEYCHELLES
VICTORIA
Aldabra Is. (to Seychelles)
Amirante Is. (to Seychelles)
Mombasa
Dar es Salaam
COMOROS
MORONI
Mayotte (to France)
MADAGASCAR
ANTANANARIVO
Zambezi
Beira
Limpopo
Durban

Cape of Good Hope
Cape Town

Madagascar Basin

Atlantic-Indian Basin

Southwest Indian Ridge

Southeast Indian Ridge

Central Indian Ridge

MAURITIUS
PORT LOUIS
RÉUNION (to France)
Le Port

MAURITIUS
P 1.1 million
L English

MADAGASCAR
P 12.8 million
L Malagasy, French

PEOPLE
Many Madagascans are descended from Indonesians who crossed the Indian Ocean. Their language, Malagasy, is Malay-Indonesian in origin.

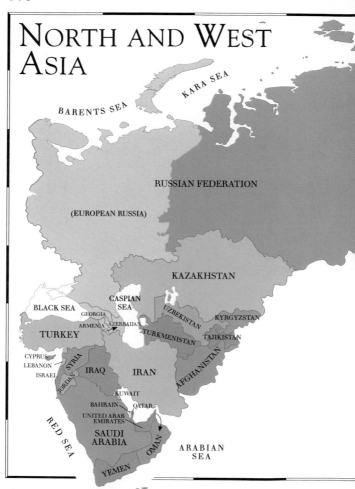

NORTH AND WEST ASIA

BARENTS SEA

KARA SEA

RUSSIAN FEDERATION

(EUROPEAN RUSSIA)

KAZAKHSTAN

CASPIAN SEA

BLACK SEA

GEORGIA

ARMENIA AZERBAIJAN

UZBEKISTAN

KYRGYZSTAN

TURKEY

TURKMENISTAN

TAJIKISTAN

CYPRUS

LEBANON

SYRIA

ISRAEL

JORDAN

IRAQ

IRAN

AFGHANISTAN

KUWAIT

BAHRAIN

QATAR

UNITED ARAB EMIRATES

RED SEA

SAUDI ARABIA

OMAN

ARABIAN SEA

YEMEN

ARCTIC OCEAN

LAPTEV SEA

EAST SIBERIAN SEA

BERING SEA

SEA OF OKHOTSK

NORTH AND WEST ASIA

Asia is the largest continent in the world, occupying nearly one-third of the world's total land area. In the south, the Arabian Peninsula is mostly hot, dry desert. In the north lie cold deserts, treeless plains called steppes, and the largest needleleaf forest in the world, which stretches from Siberia to northern Europe.

TURKEY AND CYPRUS

BRIDGING THE CONTINENTS of Europe and Asia, Turkey was once the centre of the Ottoman Empire, which controlled a quarter of Europe. Cyprus became independent from the UK in 1960, but was invaded by Turkey in 1974. Southern Cyprus is Greek; Northern Cyprus is still occupied by Turkey.

TURKEY
P 59.6 million
L Turkish

Map labels:
BULGARIA
GREECE
Bosporus
Zongulda
Istanbul
Sea of Marmara
Izmit
Dardanelles
Adapaza
Gallipoli
Bursa
Sakary
Balikesir
Eskişehir
Kütahya
T U
Manisa
AEGEAN SEA
Izmir
L. Eğridir
Ephesus
Pamukkale
Isparta
Kuşadasi
Denizli
L. Beyşehir
Antalya
MEDITERRANEA

INDUSTRY

Wheat, corn, sugar beets, nuts, fruit, cotton, tobacco, tourism. Carpet-weaving is a centuries-old tradition. Figs and peaches are grown on the coast of the Mediterranean.

ENVIRONMENT

Turkey's dam-building projects on the Tigris and Euphrates Rivers have met with disapproval from Syria and Iraq, whose own rivers will have reduced flow as a result.

PEOPLE

The Kurds are Turkey's main minority group and one of the largest groups of stateless people in the world. Their homeland, Kurdistan, straddles three countries: Turkey, Iraq, and Iran. Kurds are fighting for the recognition of their rights within Turkey.

E F G H

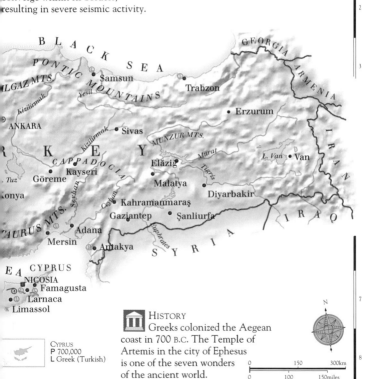

NATURAL FEATURES
Turkey lies within the Alpine-Himalayan mountain belt. The Arabian, African, Eurasian, Aegean, and Turkish plates all converge within its borders, resulting in severe seismic activity.

CLIMATE
Coastal regions of Turkey and Cyprus have a Mediterranean climate. The Turkish interior has cold, snowy winters and hot, dry summers.

BLACK SEA

PONTIC MOUNTAINS

ILGAZ MTS.

● Samsun

● Trabzon

GEORGIA

ARMENIA

Kızılırmak

Yeşil

● ANKARA

Kızılırmak

● Sivas

● Erzurum

MUNZUR MTS.

Murat

L. Van ● Van

IRAN

R   K   E   Y

CAPPADOCIA

Tuz

Göreme ● Kayseri

● Elazig

Tigris

Konya

Seyhan

● Malatya

● Diyarbakir

TAURUS MTS.

Ceyhan

● Kahramanmaraş

Gaziantep ● Şanlıurfa

Euphrates

● Adana

Mersin ● Antakya

S   Y   R   I   A

IRAQ

EA CYPRUS

● NICOSIA

● Famagusta

● Larnaca

* Limassol

HISTORY
Greeks colonized the Aegean coast in 700 B.C. The Temple of Artemis in the city of Ephesus is one of the seven wonders of the ancient world.

N

CYPRUS
P 700,000
L Greek (Turkish)

0   150   300km
0   100   150miles

E F G H

THE NEAR EAST

AT THE JUNCTION of Africa, Asia, and Europe, the Near East is a mosaic of deserts, mountains, and fertile valleys. After centuries of conflict over territory, there is now some hope for peace in the region. In 1994, Israel and Jordan ended 46 years of hostility, and Israel withdrew from Gaza and Jericho. Israel and Palestine still struggle towards a negotiated peace, despite constant setbacks.

INDUSTRY
Oil, potash, cotton, fruit. Water is in short supply in this region and special irrigation techniques are used in order to avoid waste. Syria's main cash crop is cotton.

LEBANON
P 2.9 million
L Arabic

ISRAEL
P 5.4 million
L Hebrew, Arabic

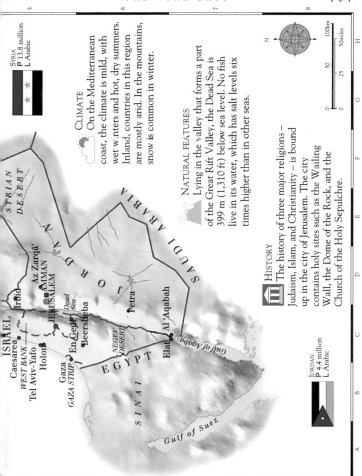

SYRIA
P 13.8 million
L Arabic

CLIMATE
On the Mediterranean coast, the climate is mild, with wet winters and hot, dry summers. Inland, countries in this region are mostly arid. In the mountains, snow is common in winter.

NATURAL FEATURES
Lying in the valley that forms a part of the Great Rift Valley, the Dead Sea is 399 m (1,310 ft) below sea level. No fish live in its water, which has salt levels six times higher than in other seas.

HISTORY
The history of three major religions – Judaism, Islam, and Christianity – is bound up in the city of Jerusalem. The city contains holy sites such as the Wailing Wall, the Dome of the Rock, and the Church of the Holy Sepulchre.

JORDAN
P 4.4 million
L Arabic

N

0   50   100km
0   25   50miles

THE MIDDLE EAST

ISLAM WAS FOUNDED in A.D. 570 in Mecca, Saudi Arabia, and spread throughout the Middle East, where today it is the main religion. Oil has brought wealth to the region but in 1991, the area was devastated by the Gulf War.

IRAQ
P 19.9 million
L Arabic

INDUSTRY
Oil, natural gas, fishing, carpet-weaving, offshore banking. Saudi Arabia has the world's largest oil reserves. Over 60 per cent of the world's desalination plants are used in this region to make sea water drinkable.

SAUDI ARABIA
P 16.5 million
L Arabic

KUWAIT
P 1.8 million
L Arabic

CLIMATE
Most of the countries in this region are semi-arid, with low rainfall. Inland, summer temperatures can reach 48°C (119°F) with winter temperatures falling to freezing.

BAHRAIN
P 500,000
L Arabic

QATAR
P 500,000
L Arabic

Mecca
⊕⊙●●
Jedda

HISTORY
Ancient civilizations developed about 5,500 years ago in Mesopotamia, between the Tigris and Euphrates Rivers. The Sumerian civilization had advanced methods of irrigation, sophisticated architecture, and a form of writing called cuneiform.

UNITED ARAB EMIRATES
P 1.7 million
L Arabic

YEMEN
P 13 million
L Arabic

Hode
Al Mul
Bab el M

IRAN
P 63.2 million
L Farsi

E   G   H

ASPIAN SEA

TURKMENISTAN

L. Urmia
Ardabīl
Rasht

Mosul
Irbīl
Kirkūk   Zanjān   Sarī
As Sulaymānīyah   Sanandaj   Semnān

ELBURZ MTS.

I R A Q   Bakhtarān Qom   Semnān
BAGHDAD   Īlām   Arāk
Karbala Al-Hillah Dezfūl   Mashhad
An-Najaf   Eşfahān

DASHT-E KAVIR

SYRIA
TIGRIS

Euphrates
Al 'Amārah
An Nāşirīyah   Ahvāz   Yazd

RIAN
DESERT

AFUD   Al-Basrah
                 Ābādān
KUWAIT CITY   Yāsūj
                 KUWAIT Shīrāz   Kermān

DASHT-E LUT

Z A G R O S   M T S.

Buraydah   Zāhedān

Ad
Dammām   Bandar-e Abbās

N E J D

RIYADH   MANAMA BAHRAIN
A D   D A H N A   Jaz Mūrian
Al Hufūf   DOHA   Strait of   Salt Lake
         QATAR   Hormuz   Khasab
                           (to Oman)
ABU DHABI   Dubai

SAUDI   UNITED ARAB
                 EMIRATES
ARABIA   AL FUJAIRAH   MUSCAT

The Gulf

RUB' AL KHALI

O M A N

OMAN
P 1.7 million
L Arabic

RAMLAT AS SAB' ATAYN   Masīrah I.
SAN'A   Gulf of Masīrah

Y E M E N
HADHRAMAUT

Aden

A R A B I A N   S E A

PAKISTAN

AFGHANISTAN

Gulf of Oman

N

0   300   600km
0   150   300miles

E   F   G   H

CENTRAL ASIA

FOR CENTURIES, many people in central Asia lived in mountains as nomads, or in cities that sprung up along the Silk Road. When the region came under Soviet rule, industry was developed and irrigation schemes made farming possible.

INDUSTRY
Cotton, gold, gas, sulphur, mercury, opium, hydroelectricity. Uzbekistan has the largest single gold mine in the world. Tajikistan has 14 per cent of the world's known uranium resources.

HISTORY
In the early 1900s, most of this region, except for Afghanistan, came under Soviet rule, which restricted the use of local languages and Islam. Today, these newly independent countries are resuming the religions, languages, and traditions of their past.

TURKMENISTAN
P 4 million
L Turkmen, Russian

ENVIRONMENT
Crop irrigation draws water from the Amu Darya river, reducing the amount of water flowing into the Aral Sea. By the year 2000, the Sea will have shrunk to an estimated third of its original size.

USTYURT PLATEAU

ARAL SEA

TURAN LOWLAND

L. Sarykamysh

Nukus

UZB

Zaliv Kara-Bogaz-Gol

Tashauz

Urgench

Krasnovodsk

CASPIAN SEA

Nebit Dag

TURKMENISTAN

ASHKABAD

I R A N

Karaku

Tedzhen

Murgab

Her

A F

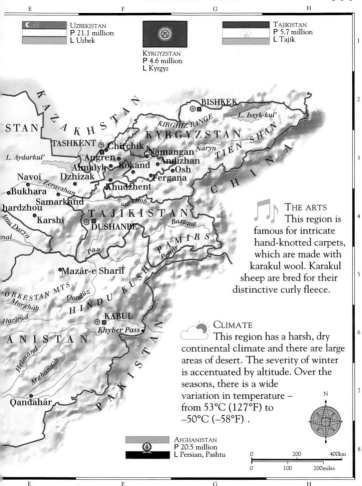

UZBEKISTAN
P 21.1 million
L Uzbek

KYRGYZSTAN
P 4.6 million
L Kyrgyz

TAJIKISTAN
P 5.7 million
L Tajik

THE ARTS
This region is famous for intricate hand-knotted carpets, which are made with karakul wool. Karakul sheep are bred for their distinctive curly fleece.

CLIMATE
This region has a harsh, dry continental climate and there are large areas of desert. The severity of winter is accentuated by altitude. Over the seasons, there is a wide variation in temperature – from 53°C (127°F) to –50°C (–58°F) .

AFGHANISTAN
P 20.5 million
L Persian, Pashtu

N

0   200   400km
0   100   200miles

THE RUSSIAN FEDERATION AND KAZAKHSTAN

EXTENDING FROM the frozen north to the central Asian deserts in the south, the Ural Mountains separate European and Asian Russia. Independent since 1991, Kazakhstan is one of the most underpopulated countries in the world.

CLIMATE
Kazakhstan has a continental climate. Winter temperatures in Russia vary little from north to south, but fall sharply in the east, especially in Siberia.

PEOPLE
There are 57 nationalities with their own territories within the Russian Federation. A further 95 groups have no territories of their own, although these groups make up only six per cent of the population.

FINLAND
BARENTS SEA
Murmansk
ESTONIA
LATVIA
St. Petersburg
Arkhangel'sk
Pskov
Novgorod
BELORUSSIA
Smolensk
Yaroslavl'
MOSCOW
Tula
Ryazan'
Kirov
UKRAINE
Voronezh
Penza
Kazan'
Izhevsk
Perm'
URAL MOUNTAINS
Ob'
WE
Rostov-na-Donu
Simbirsk
Naberezhnyye Cheln
Saratov
Samara
Yekaterinburg
Krasnodar
Tol'yatti
Ufa
Volgograd
Ural'sk
Orenburg
Chelyabinsk
GEORGIA
Astrakhan
Ural
Kustanai
Omsk
CASPIAN SEA
Aktyubinsk
Ishim
Grozny
Atyrau
Emba
ASTANA
UZBEKISTAN
KIRGHIZ STEPPE
L. Tengiz
Karaganda
ARAL SEA
KAZAKHSTAN
TURKMENISTAN
Kzyl-Orda
L. Balkhas
Syr Darya
Chu
Ili
UZBEKISTAN
Shymkent
Almaty
C

KAZAKHSTAN
P 17.2 million
L Kazakh

E   F   G   H

Bering St.

Wrangel I.

CHUKCHI SEA

Anadyr'   C. Navarin

HISTORY
Kazakhstan was absorbed by Russia in
he 19th century, when Russians began to
ettle the land used by nomadic Kazakhs.
ettlement and industrial development
ncreased after 1917.

EAST SIBERIAN SEA

Ayon Is.   Kolyma

Bear Is.

BERING SEA

New Siberian Is.

Cape Olyutorskiy

ya   Severnaya
ya   Zemlya   Bolshevik I.

Karaginskiy Is.

C. Chelyuskin

LAPTEV SEA   Olenëk   Olekma

KAMCHATKA

Belyy Is.

TAYMYR PENINSULA   L. Taymyr   Anabar

Korkodon

Petropavlovsk
-Kamchatskiy

Pyasina   Khatanga

Magadan

GYDA   CENTRAL
ENINSULA   SIBERIAN
PLATEAU   Noril'sk

Lena

C. Lopatka
Paramushir Is.

SULA   PUTORANA   RUSSIAN

Vilyuy   Yakutsk   SEA OF OKHOTSK
C. Yelizavety

khodka   MTS.
RIAN   FEDERATION

Lower-Tunguska   Maya

Pur   Ta   Yenisey

SIBERIA   Amga   Aldan

Sakhalin

Vakh   Stony-Tunguska

Olëkma

Ob'   Ket'   Angara

Vitim   Zeya Res.   Yuzhno -
Sakhalinsk

STANOVOY RANGE

Tomsk   L. Baikal   Blagoveshchensk   Khabarovsk

Novosibirsk   Ob   Shilka   SEA OF JAPAN
naul   Novokuznetsk

Biysk   Abakan   Angarsk   Ulan-Ude   C H I N A

ipalatinsk   Kyzyl   rkutsk   Vladivostok

M O N G O L I A   NORTH
KOREA

N

INDUSTRY
Oil, gas, coal, gold, diamonds.
Mineral-rich Kazakhstan has the
world's largest chromium mine. Siberia
has large gas, coal, and oil fields.

RUSSIAN
FEDERATION
P 149.2 million
L Russian

0   600   1200km

0   300   600miles

E   F   G   H

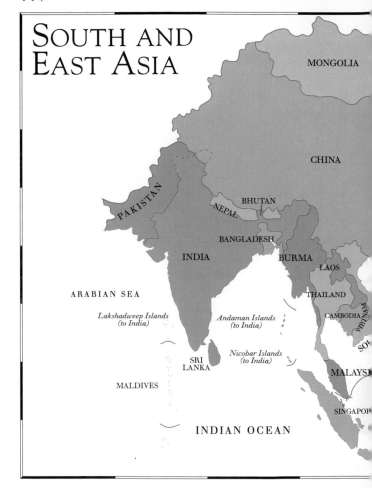

SOUTH AND EAST ASIA

MONGOLIA

CHINA

PAKISTAN

BHUTAN

NEPAL

BANGLADESH

INDIA

BURMA

LAOS

THAILAND

CAMBODIA

VIETNAM

ARABIAN SEA

*Lakshadweep Islands
(to India)*

*Andaman Islands
(to India)*

SRI
LANKA

*Nicobar Islands
(to India)*

MALAYSIA

MALDIVES

SINGAPORE

INDIAN OCEAN

SO

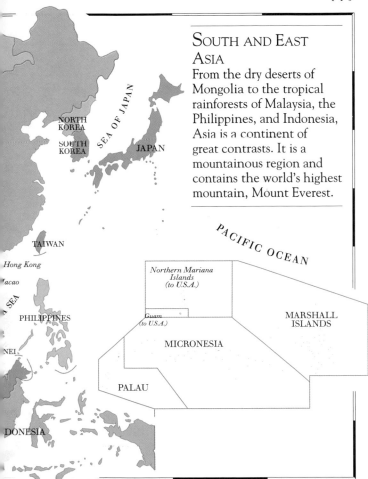

SOUTH AND EAST ASIA

From the dry deserts of Mongolia to the tropical rainforests of Malaysia, the Philippines, and Indonesia, Asia is a continent of great contrasts. It is a mountainous region and contains the world's highest mountain, Mount Everest.

NORTH KOREA

SOUTH KOREA

SEA OF JAPAN

JAPAN

TAIWAN

Hong Kong

Macao

A SEA

PHILIPPINES

NEI

DONESIA

PACIFIC OCEAN

Northern Mariana Islands
(to U.S.A.)

Guam
(to U.S.A.)

MICRONESIA

MARSHALL ISLANDS

PALAU

THE INDIAN SUBCONTINENT

SEPARATED FROM THE rest of Asia by the Himalayas, India is the second most populated country after China. It is estimated that India's population will overtake that of China by 2030. To the north, Nepal and Bhutan lie nestled in the Himalayas between China and India. To the south lies Sri Lanka, once known as Ceylon.

AFGHANISTAN

IRAN

CHAGAI HILLS

TOBA KAKAR RANGE

PAKISTAN

MAKRAN

Indus

THA

Hyderabad

Karachi

ARABIAN SEA

Gulf of Kutch

Rajkot

Gulf of Khambh

INDUSTRY
Tea, jute, iron, cut diamonds, cotton, rice, sugar cane, textiles. Bangladesh exports 80 per cent of the world's jute fibre. Sri Lanka is the largest tea exporter in the world. Pakistan is a major exporter of rice.

HISTORY
In 1947, when India gained independence, religious differences led to the creation of two countries – Hindu India and Muslim Pakistan. In 1971, a short civil war broke out between East and West Pakistan and East Pakistan became Bangladesh.

INDIA
P 896.6 million
L Hindi, English

NATURAL FEATURES
The Himalayas were formed as a result of a violent crumpling of the Earth's crust. Frequent earthquakes indicate that the process is continuing. The highest peaks in the world, including Mount Everest, are in this mountain system.

N

| 0 | 350 | 700km |
| 0 | 200 | 400miles |

PAKISTAN
P 128.1 million
L Urdu

NEPAL
P 21.1 million
L Nepali

BHUTAN
P 1.7 million
L Dzongkha

BANGLADESH
P 122.2 million
L Bengali

SRI LANKA
P 17.9 million
L Sinhalese,
Tamil

CLIMATE

Sri Lanka and southern India are tropical, with little seasonal variation in temperature. The north has a cold alpine climate. Cyclones regularly build up in the Bay of Bengal, and Bangladesh is often flooded during the monsoon.

CHINA AND MONGOLIA

ISOLATED FROM THE western world for centuries, the Chinese were the first to develop the compass, paper, gunpowder, porcelain, and silk. Three autonomous regions lie within western China – Inner Mongolia, Xinjiang, and Tibet. The Gobi desert in vast Mongolia is the world's most northern desert.

PEOPLE
Han Chinese make up 93 per cent of China's population. China has relaxed its 1979 one-child policy for minority groups, such as the Mongolians, Tibetans, and Muslim Uygurs, after some groups faced near extinction.

HISTORY
Tibet was invaded by China in 1950. The Chinese destroyed Tibet's traditional agricultural society and brutally repressed Buddhism. In 1959 there were more than 6,000 Buddhist monasteries – by 1980, only 179 remained.

KAZAKHSTAN

L. Uvs

Har Us L.

TELI MTS.

XINJIANG UIGHUR
Ürümqi

AUTONOMOUS

KYRGYZSTAN

TIEN MTS.

Tarim

L. Bosten

REGION

Tarim Basin

Lop Nur

TAKLA MAKAN
DESERT

AFGHANISTAN

KARAKORAM MTS.

PAKISTAN

ALTUN MTS.

C H

KUNLUN MTS.

BAYA

Aksai
Chin
(Controlled by
China, claimed
by India)

TIBETAN

AUTONOMOUS

TANGGULA MTS.

Demchok
(Claimed by both
China and India)

REGION

INDIA

GANGDISE RANGE

Brahmaputra (Yarlung Zangbo)

Lhasa

HIMALAYA

NEPAL

BHUTAN

IN

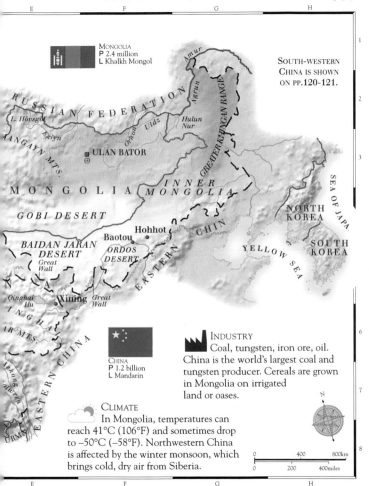

SOUTH-WESTERN CHINA IS SHOWN ON PP.120–121.

MONGOLIA
P 2.4 million
L Khalkh Mongol

RUSSIAN FEDERATION

L. Hövsgöl

HANGAYN MTS.

Egiyn

Orhon   Uldz

ULAN BATOR

Amur

Argun

Hulun Nur

GREATER KHINGAN RANGE

M O N G O L I A

INNER MONGOLIA

GOBI DESERT

BAIDAN JARAN DESERT
Great Wall

ORDOS DESERT

Baotou

Hohhot

E A S T E R N   C H I N A

SEA OF JAPA

NORTH KOREA

SOUTH KOREA

YELLOW SEA

Qinghai Hu

Xining   Great Wall

QINGHAI

NAR MTS.

URMS.

Mekong

Anwen

EASTERN CHINA

CHINA
P 1.2 billion
L Mandarin

INDUSTRY

Coal, tungsten, iron ore, oil. China is the world's largest coal and tungsten producer. Cereals are grown in Mongolia on irrigated land or oases.

CLIMATE

In Mongolia, temperatures can reach 41°C (106°F) and sometimes drop to –50°C (–58°F). Northwestern China is affected by the winter monsoon, which brings cold, dry air from Siberia.

N

0   400   800km
0   200   400miles

CHINA AND KOREA

ONE-FIFTH of the world's population lives in China – mostly in the eastern part of the country. Annexed to Japan in 1910, Korea was divided between the U.S.A. and Communist Russia after World War II. North and South Korea were formed in 1948.

NORTH-WESTERN CHINA IS SHOWN ON PP. 118–119.

RUSSIAN FEDERATION

LESSER XINGAN MTS.

Amur

MANCHURIA

Qiqihar

Harbin

Jilin

Changchun

Ch'ŏngjin

NORTH KOREA

Fushun

Shenyang

Anshan

Changchun

Sinŭiju

PYONGYANG

Namp'o

SEOUL

Inch'ŏn

Taegu

Pusan

SOUTH KOREA

Cheju

Korea Strait

CHINA SEA

Dalian

Tangshan

Bo Hai

YELLOW SEA

Shandong Pen.

Qingdao

Zibo

Jinan

Zaozhuang

Wuxi

Shanghai

Nanjing

Hangzhou

CHINA

EASTERN

PEKING

Datong

Tientsin

Shijiazhuang

Taiyuan

Handan

Zhengzhou

Luoyang

Xi'an

QIN LING

Huainan

Hefei

Great Wall

Yellow River

Lanzhou

NINGXIA HUI AUTONOMOUS REGION

WESTERN CHINA

MONGOLIA

Great Wall

Chengdu

Dadu He

Yalong

Yangtze

Jins

NORTH KOREA
P 23.1 million
L Korean

SOUTH KOREA
P 44.5 million
L Korean

TAIWAN
P 20.8 million
L Mandarin

HISTORY
On 1 July, 1997, Britain returned Hong Kong to China where it is now run as a Special Administrative Region.

COMMUNICATIONS
South Korea has one of the world's best public transport systems. Buses, trains, boats, and planes are all integrated in one timetable.

INDUSTRY
Rice, electronics, wheat, finance, textiles. Hong Kong has the busiest container port in the world. Taiwan is the world's leading producer of watches, computers, televisions, and track shoes.

PEOPLE
Korea has been inhabited by one ethnic group for 2,000 years and even today those with the same surname group may not marry each other. Most Taiwanese are descendants of the Chinese supporters of the deposed Ming dynasty, who migrated in 1644.

CLIMATE
Southern South Korea and Taiwan have a tropical monsoon climate similar to that of southern China. North Korea has a continental climate.

CHINA
P 1.2 billion
L Mandarin

0   300   600km
0   150   300miles

JAPAN

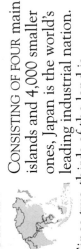

CONSISTING OF FOUR main islands and 4,000 smaller ones, Japan is the world's leading industrial nation. Since two-thirds of the land is mountainous, the majority of people live on the coast. Japan has about 1,500 minor earthquakes a year, but severe earthquakes, such as the one in Kobe in 1994, occur every few years. Underwater earthquakes sometimes cause huge surge waves, or *tsunami*, along Japan's Pacific coast.

INDUSTRY

Fishing, ship building, motor vehicles, computers, televisions, high-tech electronics. Motor vehicles are Japan's biggest export, and its stock exchange ranks second in the world. Japan excels at producing miniature electronic goods.

HISTORY

Japan was once ruled by warlords called *shoguns*, who discouraged contact with the outside world. In 1639, Japan cut ties with other nations and ordered all Europeans to leave, except the Dutch who were allowed one trading ship per year.

Habomai Is.
Kunashir
Ekaterina Strait
Kurile Islands

SEA OF OKHOTSK

La Pérouse Strait

ISHIKARI MTS.

Hokkaido

HIDAKA MTS.

Ishikari
Ishikari Bay
Sapporo
Uchiura Bay
Tsugaru Strait

OU MTS.

Sendai
Mogami

SEA OF JAPAN

Ojinno
Toyama Bay

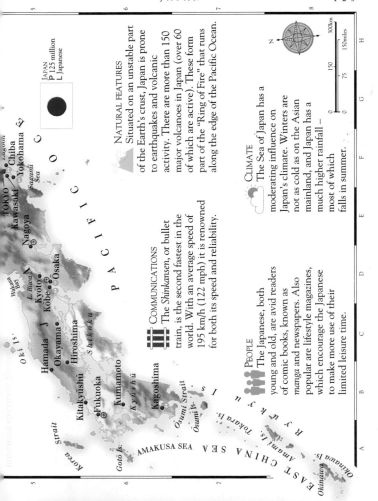

JAPAN
P 125 million
L Japanese

NATURAL FEATURES

Situated on an unstable part of the Earth's crust, Japan is prone to earthquakes and volcanic activity. There are more than 150 major volcanoes in Japan (over 60 of which are active). These form part of the "Ring of Fire" that runs along the edge of the Pacific Ocean.

CLIMATE

The Sea of Japan has a moderating influence on Japan's climate. Winters are not as cold as on the Asian mainland, and Japan has a much higher rainfall – most of which falls in summer.

COMMUNICATIONS

The *Shinkansen*, or bullet train, is the second fastest in the world. With an average speed of 195 km/h (122 mph) it is renowned for both its speed and reliability.

PEOPLE

The Japanese, both young and old, are avid readers of comic books, known as *manga* and newspapers. Also popular are lifestyle magazines, which encourage the Japanese to make more use of their limited leisure time.

MAINLAND SOUTHEAST ASIA

FOR MOST of its history, Thailand has been an independent kingdom. Malaysia includes 11 states on the mainland (Malaya), as well as Sabah and Sarawak in Borneo. Cambodia, Laos, and Vietnam have suffered from years of civil war. Burma has become more and more isolated from the world by its repressive government.

BURMA (MYANMAR)
P 44.6 million
L Burmese (Myanmar)

LAOS
P 4.6 million
L Lao

CHINA

INDIA

BURMA

B'DESH

KUMON RANGE

CHIN HILLS

Chindwin

Irrawaddy

Monywa
Mandalay
Amarapura
Sagaing
Pakokku
Paunggyi
L. Inle
Salween
Minbu
Pyinmana
Prome
Sandoway
Sitta

Bay of Bengal

Chiang Mai

LAOS

Mekong

Mekong

Nam Ou

Louang Phrabang

Nam O

Black R.
Viet Tri
Red R.
L. Thac Ba
Thai Nguyen

HANOI
V

Hong Gai
Hai Phong
Nam Dinh
Thanh
Hoa
Vinh

Gulf of Tongking

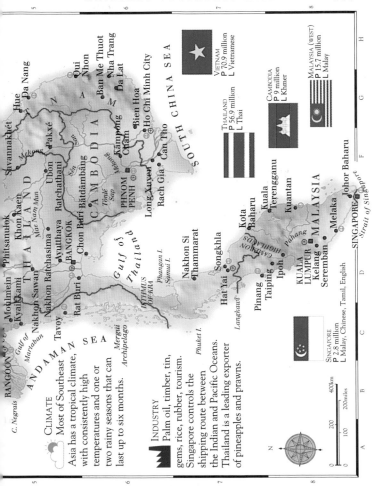

C. Negrais

RANGOON (Yangon)

Moulmein

Kyaikkami

ANDAMAN SEA

Gulf of
Martaban

Tavoy

Mergui
Archipelago

Phuket I.

C L I M A T E
Most of Southeast
Asia has a tropical climate,
with consistently high
temperatures and one or
two rainy seasons that can
last up to six months.

I N D U S T R Y
Palm oil, timber, tin,
gems, rice, rubber, tourism.
Singapore controls the
shipping route between
the Indian and Pacific Oceans.
Thailand is a leading exporter
of pineapples and prawns.

Savannakhét

Hue

Da Nang

Qui
Nhon

Ban Me Thuot

Nha Trang

Da Lat

Pakxé

Mekong

Sekong

L A O S

V I E T N A M

Phitsanulok

Khon Kaen

Nakhon Sawan

T H A I L A N D

Mae Nam Mun

Ubon

Ratchathani

Ayutthaya

Nakhon Ratchasima

BANGKOK

Chon Buri

Rat Buri

Phangan I.

Samui I.

Gulf of
Thailand

Nakhon Si
Thammarat

ISTHMUS
OF KRA

Bâtdâmbâng

Tônlé
Sap

C A M B O D I A

PHNOM
PENH

Stung Sen

Mekong

Bien Hoa

Kâmpóng
Cham

Ho Chi Minh City

Long Xuyen

Rach Gia

Can Tho

S O U T H   C H I N A   S E A

Hat Yai

Songkhla

Langkawi

Pinang

Taiping

Ipoh

Kota
Baharu

Kuala
Terengganu

Kuantan

CAMERON
HIGHLANDS

Pahang

M A L A Y S I A

KUALA
LUMPUR

Kelang

Seremban

Melaka

Johor Baharu

SINGAPORE

Strait of Singapore

VIETNAM
P 70.9 million
L Vietnamese

THAILAND
P 56.9 million
L Thai

CAMBODIA
P 9 million
L Khmer

MALAYSIA (WEST)
P 15.7 million
L Malay

SINGAPORE
P 2.8 million
L Malay, Chinese, Tamil, English

N

0   200   400km
0   100   200miles

MARITIME SOUTHEAST ASIA

SCATTERED BETWEEN the Indian and Pacific Oceans are thousands of tropical mountainous islands. Once called the East Indies, Indonesia was ruled by the Dutch for 350 years. More than half of its 13,677 islands are still uninhabited. The Philippines lie on the "Ring of Fire", and are subject to earthquakes and volcanic activity. Borneo is shared among Indonesia, Malaysia, and Brunei.

BRUNEI
P 300,000
L Malay

PHIL

Balabac Strait

SOUTH CHINA SEA

Kota Kinabalu

BANDAR SERI BEGAWAN

BRUNEI

SABA

MALAYSIA (EAST)

Rajang

SARAWAK

Natuna R.

Anambas Is.

Natuna Is.

Medan

Simeulue

L. Toba

Strait of Singapore

Kuching

B o r n e o

Nias

Sumatra

Lingga

Singkep

Pontianak

Kapuas

MULLER MTS.

Samarinda

Balikpapan

Padang

Batanghari

Bangka

Jambi

Mendawai

Barito

Siberut

BARISAN MTS.

Palembang

Belitung

Banjarmasin

Tanjungkarang

JAVA SEA

I N

JAKARTA

Cirebon

Semarang

D

Bogor

Bandung

Kediri

Surabaya

Jember

Yogyakarta

Malang

Ba

Java

Denpasar

Lombok

I N D I A N

O C E A N

N

0   300   600km
0   150   300miles

MALAYSIA (EAST)
SABAH and SARAWAK
P 3.4 million
L Malay

PHILIPPINES
P 66.5 million
L Filipino, English

INDUSTRY
Palm oil, timber, rice, oil, natural gas, copper, chrome, tourism. Malaysia is the largest producer of palm oil and computer disk-drives. Indonesia is a major exporter of natural gas.

ENVIRONMENT
Logging, especially in Borneo and the Philippines, is a problem in the region. Forest communities, like the Malaysian Penan, are being destroyed. Some tree species are near extinction.

CLIMATE
Countries situated around the equator are hot and humid all year. Variations in climate are related to latitude.

INDONESIA
P 194.6 million
L Bahasa Indonesia

PACIFIC OCEAN

THE LARGEST AND deepest ocean, the Pacific covers a greater area of the Earth's surface than all the land areas together. Its deepest point – 11,033 m (36,197ft) – is deep enough to cover Mount Everest. Melanesia, Micronesia, and Polynesia are the main inner Pacific island groups.

MICRONESIA
P 101,000
L English

NAURU
P 10,000
L Nauruan, English

NATURAL FEATURES

Some Pacific islands are coral atolls – ring-shaped islands or chains of islands surrounding a lagoon. They are formed when coral builds up on a sunken bank or on a volcano crater in the open sea.

SOLOMON
ISLANDS
P 400,000
L English

VANUATU
P 155,000
L Bislama,
English, French

ENVIRONMENT

Nuclear testing by the U.S.A. and France has dangerously polluted areas in the South Pacific. Countries such as Japan, Australia, and New Zealand want the region made into a nuclear-free zone.

FIJI
P 700,000
L English

N

| 0 | | 1500 | | 3000km |
| 0 | 750 | | 1500miles | |

ARC

SEA OF
OKHOTSK

ASIA

Kurile Is.
Kurile Trench

SEA OF JAPAN

Kōbe • Yokohama

Shanghai •

NORTHERN
MARIANAS IS.
(to U.S.A.)

• Hong Kong

GUAM
(to U.S.A.)

Manila •

MARSHAL
ISLAN

FEDERATED
STATES
OF MICRONES

MICRONE

PALAU
(to U.S.A.)

SOUTH
EAST ASIA

NAURU

ARAFURA
SEA

SOLOMO
IS.

CORAL
SEA

VANUA

NEW
CALEDONI
(to Franc

AUSTRALIA

Great
Barrier
Reef

Sydney •

TASMAN
SEA

SOU

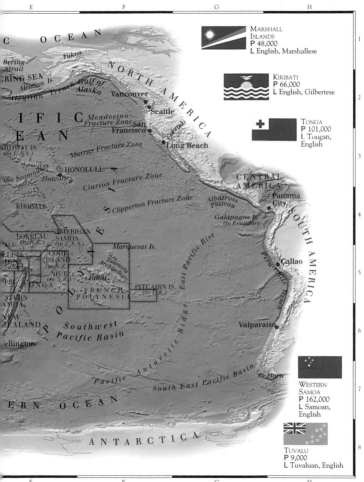

E   F   G   H

OCEAN

Yukon

Bering Strait

RING SEA

NORTH AMERICA

Aleutian Is.

Aleutian Trench *Gulf of Alaska*

IFIC

Vancouver

Seattle

Mendocino Fracture Zone

San Francisco

Colorado

EAN

Murray Fracture Zone

Long Beach

MIDWAY IS. (to U.S.A.)

HONOLULU

The Seamounts *Hawaii*

Clarion Fracture Zone

CENTRAL AMERICA

KIRIBATI

Clipperton Fracture Zone

Albatross Plateau

Panama City

Galápagos Is. (to Ecuador)

SOUTH AMERICA

TOKELAU (to N.Z.)

AMERICAN SAMOA (to U.S.A.)

Marquesas Is.

COOK ISLAND (to N.Z.)

NIUE (to N.Z.)

Tuamotu Archipelago

Tahiti

FRENCH POLYNESIA

PITCAIRN IS. (to U.K.)

East Pacific Rise

Callao

Peru–Chile Trench

POLYNESIA

WALLIS & FUTUNA (to France)

TONGA

WESTERN SAMOA

NEW ZEALAND

Southwest Pacific Basin

Valparaiso

Wellington

Pacific–Antarctic Ridge

South East Pacific Basin

C. Horn

ERN OCEAN

ANTARCTICA

MARSHALL ISLANDS
P 48,000
L English, Marshallese

KIRIBATI
P 66,000
L English, Gilbertese

TONGA
P 101,000
L Tongan, English

WESTERN SAMOA
P 162,000
L Samoan, English

TUVALU
P 9,000
L Tuvaluan, English

E   F   G   H

AUSTRALASIA

NAURU

PAPUA NEW
GUINEA

SOLOMON
ISLANDS

Coral Sea Islands
(to Australia)

VANUATU

New Caledonia
(to France)

AUSTRALIA

TASMAN SEA

NEW ZEALAN

SOUTHERN OCEAN

Auckland Islands
(to N.Z.)

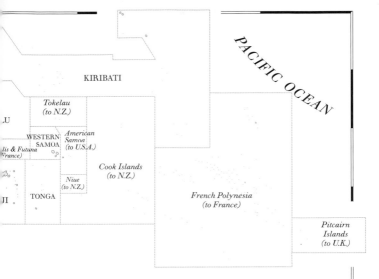

KIRIBATI

Tokelau
(to N.Z.)

,U

WESTERN
SAMOA
*American
Samoa
(to U.S.A.)*

*lis & Futuna
rance)*

Cook Islands
(to N.Z.)

*Niue
(to N.Z.)*

TONGA

French Polynesia
(to France)

JI

PACIFIC OCEAN

Pitcairn
Islands
(to U.K.)

*Chatham Island
(to N.Z.)*

AUSTRALASIA

Millions of years ago, the continent of
Australia and the islands of New Guinea
and New Zealand split away from the
other southern continents. These island
countries have many unique plants and
animals, such as Australia's marsupials,
or pouched mammals. The thousands of
islands scattered in the Pacific are either
volcanic islands or coral atolls.

AUSTRALIA AND PAPUA NEW GUINEA

THE SMALLEST, flattest, and driest continent, Australia has a landscape that varies from tropical rainforest to arid desert. Lying to the north, Papua New Guinea (PNG) is so mountainous that its tribes are isolated from each other and from the outside world.

AUSTRALIA
P 18.5 million
L English

TIMOR SEA

Joseph Bonaparte Gulf

DARWIN

ARNHEM LAND

Victoria

KIMBERLEY PLATEAU

KING LEOPOLD RANGES

Fitzroy

INDIAN OCEAN

GREAT SANDY DESERT

North West C.

HAMERSLEY RANGE

L. Mackay

L. Disappointment

Alice Springs

T

NOR

TER

L. Macleod

WESTERN

MACDONNELL RANGES

GIBSON DESERT

Dirk Hartog I.

AUSTRALIA

L. Carnegie

GREAT VICTORIA DESERT

L. Barlee

L. Moore

NULLARBOR PLAIN

A U

PERTH

C. Naturaliste

C. Leeuwin

Great Australian B.

C. Pasley

CLIMATE

Most people live in temperate zones that occur within 400 km (249 miles) of the coast in the east and southeast, and around Perth in the west. The interior, west, and south are arid; the north is tropical. PNG is tropical, yet snow falls on its highest mountains.

INDUSTRY

Coal, gold, uranium, cattle, tourism, wool, wine- and beer-making. Australia is a leading exporter of coal, iron ore, gold, bauxite, and copper, and has the largest known diamond deposit. PNG has the largest copper mine in the world and one of the largest gold mines.

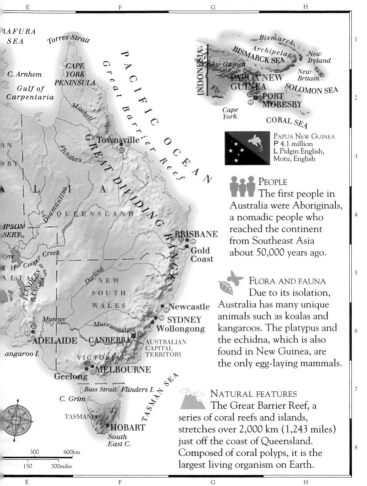

E F G H

ARAFURA
SEA

Torres Strait

Bismarck
Archipelago

BISMARCK SEA

New Guinea

New
Ireland

C. Arnhem

CAPE
YORK
PENINSULA

INDONESIA

Fly

PAPUA NEW
GUINEA

PORT
MORESBY

New
Britain

SOLOMON SEA

Gulf of
Carpentaria

Mitchell

Great Barrier Reef

PACIFIC OCEAN

*Cape
York*

CORAL SEA

Flinders

GREAT BARRIER REEF

Townsville

GREAT DIVIDING RANGE

Diamantina

QUEENSLAND

BRISBANE

Gold
Coast

Cooper Creek

Darling

NEW
SOUTH
WALES

Newcastle

SYDNEY
Wollongong

Murray

Murrumbidgee

ADELAIDE

CANBERRA

AUSTRALIAN
CAPITAL
TERRITORY

Kangaroo I.

VICTORIA

MELBOURNE

Geelong

Bass Strait *Flinders I.*

TASMAN SEA

C. Grim

TASMANIA

HOBART

*South
East C.*

EYRE

Eyre

Cooper Creek

FLINDERS RANGES

SIMPSON
DESERT

L A K E

300   600km
150   300miles

PAPUA NEW GUINEA
P 4.1 million
L Pidgin English,
Motu, English

PEOPLE
The first people in
Australia were Aboriginals,
a nomadic people who
reached the continent
from Southeast Asia
about 50,000 years ago.

FLORA AND FAUNA
Due to its isolation,
Australia has many unique
animals such as koalas and
kangaroos. The platypus and
the echidna, which is also
found in New Guinea, are
the only egg-laying mammals.

NATURAL FEATURES
The Great Barrier Reef, a
series of coral reefs and islands,
stretches over 2,000 km (1,243 miles)
just off the coast of Queensland.
Composed of coral polyps, it is the
largest living organism on Earth.

E F G H

NEW ZEALAND

ONE OF THE LAST places on Earth to be inhabited by people, New Zealand lies about halfway between the equator and the South Pole. It is made up of the main North and South Islands, separated by the Cook Strait, and numerous smaller islands. The first settlers were Maoris, who came from the Polynesian islands about 1,200 years ago.

NATURAL FEATURES

New Zealand lies on the "Ring of Fire", a band of volcanic activity that almost encircles the Pacific Ocean. New Zealand has about 400 earthquakes each year, although only about 100 are strong enough to be felt.

PEOPLE

In recent years, Maoris have protested the lack of observance of the Treaty of Waitangi, which protected their rights. About 10 per cent of the total population are Maori.

FLORA AND FAUNA

Many of New Zealand's animals have been introduced – two species of bat are the only native land mammals. New Zealand has no snakes.

Great Exhibition Bay

Great Barrier I.

Kaipara Harbour

Auckland

Bay of Plenty

Hamilton

L. Taupo

North Island

TASMAN SEA

Hawke Bay

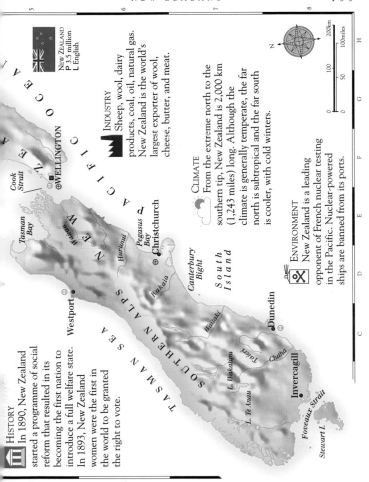

NEW ZEALAND
P 3.5 million
L English

INDUSTRY
Sheep, wool, dairy products, coal, oil, natural gas. New Zealand is the world's largest exporter of wool, cheese, butter, and meat.

CLIMATE
From the extreme north to the southern tip, New Zealand is 2,000 km (1,243 miles) long. Although the climate is generally temperate, the far north is subtropical and the far south is cooler, with cold winters.

ENVIRONMENT
New Zealand is a leading opponent of French nuclear testing in the Pacific. Nuclear-powered ships are banned from its ports.

HISTORY
In 1890, New Zealand started a programme of social reform that resulted in its becoming the first nation to introduce a full welfare state. In 1893, New Zealand women were the first in the world to be granted the right to vote.

PACIFIC OCEAN

TASMAN SEA

SOUTHERN ALPS

N E W

●WELLINGTON

Cook Strait

Tasman Bay

Westport ●

Waimea

Hurunui

Rakaia

Pegasus Bay

Christchurch ⊕

Canterbury Bight

South Island

Waitaki

Waitaki

Taieri

Clutha

Dunedin ●

L. Wakatipu

L. Te Anau

Invercargill ●

Foveaux Strait

Stewart I.

N

0   50   100   200km
0   50   100miles

Index

Grid references in the Index help find places on the map. If you look up Nairobi in the Index, you will see 96 F4. The first number, 96, is the page number on which the map of Nairobi appears. Next, find the letters and numbers which border the page and trace a line across from the letter and down from the number. This will direct you to the exact grid square in which the city of Nairobi is located.

Bafoussam Cameroon 95 C5
Baghdad Iraq 109 E3
Baguio Philippines 127 E2
Bahamas (Country) 43 E2
Bahrain (Country) 109 F5
Baia Mare Romania 76 D3
Baikal, Lake Rus.Fed.113 F6
Baja California Mexico 38 C3
Baker City USA 36 D4
Bakersfield USA 37 D7
Bakhtarān Iran 109 F2
Baku Azerbaijan 85 H7
Balaton, Lake Hungary 75 D7
Balearic Is. Spain 61 H5
Bali (I.) Indonesia 126 D8
Balikesir Turkey 104 C4
Balikpapan Indonesia 126 D6
Balkan Mts. S.E. Europe 77 D5
Balkhash, Lake Kazakhstan 112 D7
Balsas (R.) Mexico 39 F6
Baltic Sea N. Europe 52 G3/70–71 D1/80 B4
Baltimore USA 29 H2
Bamako Mali 92 D5
Ban Me Thuot Vietnam 125 G6
Banda Sea Indonesia 127 F7
Bandar Seri Begawan Brunei 126 D5
Bandar-e Abbās Iran 109 G5
Bandundu Congo (Zaire) 95 D6
Bandung Indonesia 126 C8
Bangalore India 117 E7
Bangkok Thailand 125 D5

Bangladesh (Country) 117 G4
Bangui Central African Republic 95 E5
Banja Luka Bosnia & Herzegovina 75 E6
Banjarmasin Indonesia 126 D7
Banjul Gambia 92 B5
Banská Bystrica Slovakia 71 E7
Baotou China 119 F4
Baranavichy Belorussia 81 D6
Barbados (Country) 43 H7
Barcelona Spain 61 G3
Bareilly India 111 F3
Barents Sea Arctic Ocean 51 H6/82 E3/112 D3
Bari Italy 73 G5
Barinas Venezuela 44 C3
Barnaul Rus. Fed. 113 E6
Barquisimeto Venezuela 44 D3
Barranquilla Colombia 44 B3
Barysaw Belorussia 81 F6
Basle Switzerland 68 B4
Basque Provinces Spain 61 E2
Bassein Burma 125 B5
Bata Equatorial Guinea 95 B5
Batangas Philippines 127 E2
Bătdâmbâng Cambodia 125 E6
Baton Rouge USA 28 D5
Bavaria Germany 67 F6
Bavarian Alps (Mts.) Germany 67 F7
Bayan Har Mts. China 118 D6
Beaufort Sea 22 D3/51 F3

Beaumont USA 35 H6
Béchar Algeria 88 D3
Beersheba Israel 107 C6
Beira Mozambique 99 G5/101 B6
Beirut Lebanon 106 C4
Beja Portugal 60 C6
Belém Brazil 46 F4
Belfast Northern Ireland UK 59 D5
Belgium (Country) 65
Belgrade Yugoslavia 76 B4
Belize (Country) 42 B4
Bellevue USA 36 B3
Bellingshausen Sea Antarctica 50 B4
Belmopan Belize 42 B4
Belo Horizonte Brazil 47 F6
Belorussia (Country) 81
Bengal, Bay of India/ South Asia 100 F4/ 117 G5/124 A4
Benghazi Libya 89 G3
Benin (Country) 93 F6
Berbera Somalia 91 G6
Berbérati Central African Republic 95 D5
Bergen Norway 52 F3/ 57 A5
Bergen op Zoom Netherlands 64 C4
Bering Sea Pacific Ocean 22 B4/113 H2/129 E2
Bering Strait Arctic Ocean/Pacific Ocean 22 B3/113 H1/129 E1
Berlin Germany 66 G4
Bermuda (I.) UK 52 C4
Bern Switzerland 68 B4
Bernese Alps (Mts.) Switzerland 68 B4
Beskid Mts. Poland 71 F5
Bhopal India 117 E4

Bhutan (Country) 117 G3
Bielefeld Germany 66 D4
Bien Hoa Vietnam 125 G6
Bila Tserkva Ukraine 84 D3
Birmingham UK 59 F6
Birmingham USA 29 E4
Biscay, Bay of Spain 61 E1
Bishkek Kyrgyzstan 111 G2
Bissau Guinea-Bissau 92 C4
Bitola Macedonia 77 C6
Biysk Rus. Fed. 113 E6
Black (R.) China/Vietnam 124 E4
Black Forest Germany 67 D6
Black Sea 77 H6/83 A7/ 85 G6/104 – 105
Blagoveshchensk Rus. Fed. 113 G6
Blanco, Cape USA 36 A4
Blantyre Malawi 97 F7
Bob-Dioulasso Burkina 93 E6
Bogor Indonesia 126 C7
Bogotà Colombia 44 B4
Bohemia Czech Republic 70 C6
Boise USA 32 C3
Bolivia (Country) 45 E7
Bologna Italy 72 D4
Bombay India 100 E4/ 117 E5
Bomu (R.) Central African Republic/Congo (Zaire) 95 F5
Bonifacio, Strait of Sardinia 73 B5
Bonn Germany 67 C5
Borås Sweden 57 C7
Bordeaux France 62 D6
Borneo (I.) Indonesia

101 G5/126 D5
Bosnia & Herzegovina (Country) 74 – 75
Bosporus Turkey 104 D3
Boston USA 27 G5
Bothnia, Gulf of Sweden/ Finland 57 E5
Botswana (Country) 99
Bouvet I. Norway 53 F7
Bradford UK 59 G5
Brahmaputra (var. Yarlung Zangbo) (R.) 117 H3/118 C7
Brăila Romania 76 G4
Brasília Brazil 47 F5
Braşov Romania 76 E4
Bratislava Slovakia 70 D7
Brazil (Country) 46 – 47
Brazilian Highlands (Mts.) Brazil 47 G5
Brazzaville Congo 95 D6
Brecon Beacons (Mts.) UK 59 E7
Breda Netherlands 64 D4
Bregenz Austria 68 D4
Bremen Germany 66 D3
Brest Belorussia 81 C7
Brest France 62 C3
Bridgeport USA 27 F6
Brisbane Australia 133 G4
Bristol UK 59 F7
Bristol Bay Alaska USA 22 B5
British Columbia (Province) Canada 22 D7
British Indian Ocean Territory UK 101 E5
British Virgin Is. UK 43 H5
Brittany France 62 C3
Brno Czech Republic 70 D6
Bruges Belgium 65 B5
Brunei (Country) 126 D4
Brunswick Germany

66 E4
Brussels Belgium 65 D5
Bucharest Romania 76 E4
Budapest Hungary 75 E2
Buenaventura Colombia 44 B4
Buenos Aires Argentina 49 E5/53 C6
Buenos Aires, Lake Argentina 49 C7
Buffalo USA 26 D4
Bug (R.) Poland/Ukraine 71 F3
Bujumbura Burundi 96 D4
Bukavu Congo (Zaire) 95 G6
Bukhara Uzbekistan 111 E4
Bulawayo Zimbabwe 99 E5
Bulgaria (Country) 77
Buraydah Saudi Arabia 109 E4
Burgas Bulgaria 77 F5
Burgundy France 63 F3
Burkina (Country) 93 E5
Burma (Country) 124
Bursa Turkey 104 D3
Buru (I.) Indonesia 127 F6
Burundi (Country) 96 D4
Butuan Philippines 127 F3
Buzău Romania 76 F4
Bydgoszcz Poland 71 E3

C
Cabanatuan Philippines 127 E2
Cabinda Angola 98 A3
Cabora Bassa, Lake Mozambique 98 F4
Cadiz Philippines 127 E3
Caen France 62 D2
Caesarea Israel 107 C5
Cagayan de Oro Philippines 127 F4

Eşfāhān Iran 109 G3
Eskişehir Turkey 104 D4
Essen Germany 66 C4
Estonia (Country) 80 D3
Ethiopia (Country) 91
Ethiopian Highlands
  (Mts.) Ethiopia 91 E6
Eugene USA 36 B4
Euphrates (R.) S.W. Asia
  105 F6/106 G3/109 E3
Eureka USA 37 A5
Evansville USA 31 F8
Everett USA 36 B2
Everglades, The USA
  29 F8
Evvoia Greece 79 E4
Eyre, Lake Australia
  133 E5

F
Faeroe Is. Denmark 52 E3
Fairbanks Alaska USA
  22 C4
Faisalabad Pakistan
  117 E2
Falkland Is. UK 53 C7
Famagusta Cyprus 105 E7
Farewell, Cape Greenland
  52 D3
Fargo USA 33 G2
Faro Portugal 60 C7
Farvel, Cape Greenland
  51 E8
Fergana Uzbekistan
  111 F3
Fez Morocco 88 D3
Fiji (Country) 129 E5
Finland (Country) 56 – 57
Finland, Gulf of Baltic
  Sea 57 F6/80 D2
Flinders Ranges (Mts.)
  Australia 133 E5
Flint USA 31 G5
Florence Italy 72 D4

Flores (I.) Indonesia 127 E8
Florida (State) USA 29 F6
Florida Keys USA 29 F8
Focşani Romania 76 F4
Formosa Paraguay 48 E3
Fort McMurray Canada
  23 E7
Fort Wayne USA 31 G6
Fort Worth USA 35 G5
Fortaleza Brazil 46 H4
Forth (R.) UK 58 E4
France (Country) 62 – 63
Francistown Botswana
  99 E5
Frankfort USA 29 F2
Frankfurt Germany
  67 D5
Frankivs'k Ukraine 84 C3
Franz Josef Land (Is.)
  Rus. Fed. 51 H6
Fredericton Canada 25 F7
Freetown Sierra Leone
  92 C6
Fremantle Australia
  101 G6
French Guiana France
  44 H4
French Polynesia France
  129 F5
Fresno USA 37 C7
Fukuoka Japan 123 B6
Fushun China 120 G3
Fuzhou China 121 F5

G
Gabon (Country) 95 C6
Gaborone Botswana
  99 E6
Galápagos Is. Ecuador
  129 G4
Galaţi Romania 76 F4
Galicia Poland 71 F6
Galicia Spain 60 D2
Galle Sri Lanka 117 F8

Gallipoli Turkey 104 C4
Galway Ireland 59 B5
Gambia (Country) 92 C5
Gäncä Azerbaijan 85 G7
Gangdise Range (Mts.)
  China 118 C7
Ganges (R.) India 100 F3/
  117 F3
Garda, Lake Italy 72 C3
Garonne (R.) France
  62 D6
Garoua Cameroon 94 C4
Gary USA 31 F6
Gaza Gaza Strip 107 C5
Gaza Strip 107 C5
Gaziantep Turkey 105 F6
Gdańsk Poland 71 E2
Geelong Australia 133 F7
General Santos
  Philippines 127 F4
Geneva Switzerland 68 A7
Geneva, Lake France/
  Switzerland 63 G4/68 B6
Genoa Italy 72 B4
Genoa, Gulf of Italy 72 C4
Georgetown Cayman Is.
  42 D4
Georgetown Guyana
  44 F3
Georgia (Country) 85
Georgia (State) USA 29 F5
Germany (Country) 66–67
Ghana West Africa 93 E6
Ghāt Libya 89 F5
Ghent Netherlands 65 C5
Gibraltar Gibraltar 60 D8
Gibraltar UK 52 F4/60 D8
Gibraltar, Strait of
  Morocco/Spain 60 D8/
  88 D2
Gibson Desert Australia
  132 D4
Giza Egypt 90 C3
Glasgow UK 58 E4

Kismaayo Somalia 91 F8
Kitakyūhū Japan 123 B6
Kithira (I.) Greece 79 E7
Kivu, Lake Congo (Zaire) 95 G6
Kizilirmak (R.) Turkey 105 E4
Kjølen (Mts.) Norway 56 D4
Klagenfurt Austria 69 G5
Klaipéda Lithuania 81 B5
Klamath Falls USA 37 C5
Klerksdorp South Africa 99 E6
Knud Rasmussen Land Greenland 51 F6
Kōbe Japan 123 D5/ 128 D3
Kokand Uzbekistan 111 F3
Kola Peninsula Rus. Fed. 82 D3
Kolyma (R.) Rus. Fed. 113 G3
Konya Turkey 105 E5
Korea Strait Korea/Japan 120 H3/123 A5
Kos (I.) Greece 79 G6
Košice Slovakia 71 F7
Kosovska Mitrovica Yugoslavia 77 B5
Kota Baharu Malaysia 125 E7
Kota India 117 E3
Kota Kinabalu Malaysia 126 D4
Kowloon Hong Kong 121 E6
Kraków Poland 71 E6
Kraljevo Yugoslavia 76 B4
Kramators'k Ukraine 85 E4
Krasnodar Rus. Fed. 83 A7/112 B5
Krasnovodsk

Turkmenistan 110 B3
Krasnoyarsk Rus. Fed. 113 E6
Kruševac Yugoslavia 76 C4
Kryvyy Rih Ukraine 85 E4
Kuala Lumpur Malaysia 125 E8
Kuantan Malaysia 125 E8
Kuching Malaysia 126 C5
Kumamoto Japan 123 B6
Kumanovo Macedonia 77 C5
Kumasi Ghana 93 E7
Kunlun Mts. China 118 C6
Kunming China 121 B5
Kupa (R.) Croatia 74 D5
Kupang Indonesia 127 F8
Kurile Is. E. Asia/Rus. Fed. 113 H5/122 G1/ 128 D2
Kuşadasi Turkey 104 C5
Kustanai Kazakhstan 112 D6
Kūtahya Turkey 104 D4
K'ut'aisi Georgia 85 G6
Kuujjuaq Canada 25 E2
Kuwait (Country) 109 F4
Kuwait City Kuwait 109 F4
Kwilu (R.) Angola/Congo (Zaire) 95 E7
Kyaikkami Burma 125 C5
Kyōto Japan 123 D5
Kyrgyzstan (Country) 111
Kyūshū (I.) Japan 123 B6
Kyzyl Rus. Fed. 113 E6
Kzyl-Orda Kazakhstan 112 D7

L
La Guaira Venezuela 53 C5
La Paz Bolivia 45 D7
La Paz Mexico 38 D4
La Pérouse Strait Japan 122 E1

La Serena Chile 48 B4
Labrador (Province) Canada 25 F4
Labrador Sea 25 F2/52 C3
Ladoga, Lake Rus. Fed. 82 C4
Lagos Nigeria 52 F5/93 F7
Lagos Portugal 60 C7
Lahore Pakistan 117 E2
Lake District UK 59 F5
Lakshadweep Is. India 101 E4
Lansing USA 31 G5
Lanzhou China 120 C3
Laos (Country) 124–125
Laptev Sea Rus. Fed. 51 H4/113 F3
Laredo USA 35 G7
Larisa Greece 79 E3
Larnaca Cyprus 105 E7
Las Vegas USA 34 D3
Latvia (Country) 80 D4
Lausanne Switzerland 68 B6
Laval Canada 25 E7
Le Havre France 62 D2
Le Mans France 62 D3
Le Port Réunion 101 D6
Lebanon (Country) 106
Leeds UK 59 G5
Leeuwarden Netherlands 64 F2
Leeward Is. 43 H5
Leicester UK 59 G6
Leipzig Germany 67 G5
Lena (R.) Rus. Fed. 113 F4
León Mexico 39 E5
Leskovac Yugoslavia 77 C5
Lesotho (Country) 99 E7
Lesser Antilles (Is.) 43 G7
Lesser Sunda Is. Indonesia 127 E8
Lesvos (I.) Greece 79 G3
Lewis (I.) UK 58 D2

Minorca Balearic Is. Spain
61 H4
Minsk Bclorussia 81 E6
Miskolc Hungary 75 F2
Mississippi (R.) USA
28 D3/30 D3
Mississippi (State) USA
28 D4
Missouri (R.) USA 33 E2
Missouri (State) USA 33 H5
Mitumba Mts. Congo
(Zaire) 95 G7
Mobile USA 28 D5
Mogadishu Somalia 91 G7
Mojave Desert USA 37 E7
Moldavia (Country) 84
Molucca Sea Indonesia
127 F5
Moluccas (Is.) Indonesia
127 F6
Mombasa Kenya 96 G4/
101 C5
Monaco (Country) 63 G7
Mongolia (Country)
118 – 119
Monrovia Liberia 92 C7
Mons Belgium 65 C6
Montana (State) USA 32 D2
Monte Carlo Monaco
63 G7
Montenegro (Republic)
Yugoslavia 77
Monterrey Mexico 39 F4
Montevideo Uruguay
49 E5
Montgomery USA 29 E4
Montpelier USA 27 F4
Montpellier France 63 F7
Montréal Canada 25 E7
Montserrat UK 43 H6
Monywa Burma 124 B3
Morava (R.) Czech
Republic/Slovakia 70 D7
Moravia Czech Republic

70 D6
Morocco (Country) 88
Moroni Comoros 101 C5
Moscow Rus. Fed. 83 C5/
112 C4
Mosel (R.) Germany 67 C6
Moselle (R.) France 63 G3
Mostar Bosnia &
Herzegovina 75 E7
Mosul Iraq 109 E2
Moulmein Burma 125 C5
Moundou Chad 94 D4
Mozambique (Country)
98 – 99
Muang Phitsanulok
Thailand 125 D5
Mufulira Zambia 97 C6
Mull (I.) UK 58 D3
Multan Pakistan 117 E2
Munich Germany 67 F7
Münster Germany 66 C4
Murcia Spain 61 F6
Murmansk Rus. Fed.
52 G3/82 D3/112 D3
Murray (R.) Australia
133 E6
Murrumbidgee (R.)
Australia 133 F6
Muscat Oman 109 G6
Mwanza Tanzania 96 E4
Mweru, Lake Zambia/
Congo (Zaire) 97 C5
Mykolayiv Ukraine 84 D4

N
Naberezhnyye Chelny
Rus. Fed. 83 E6/112 C5
Nacala Mozambique 98 H4
Naga Philippines 127 E2
Nagoya Japan 123 D5
Nagpur India 117 E4
Nain Canada 25 F3
Nairobi Kenya 96 F4
Nakhodka Rus. Fed.

113 E4
Nakhon Ratchasima
Thailand 125 E5
Nakhon Sawan Thailand
125 E5
Nakhon Si Thammarat
Thailand 125 D7
Nam Dinh Vietnam
124 F4
Namangan Uzbekistan
111 F3
Namibe Angola 98 A4
Namibia (Country) 99
Namp'o North Korea
120 G3
Nampula Mozambique
98 H4
Namur Belgium 65 D6
Nanchang China 121 E5
Nancy France 63 F2
Nanjing China 120 F4
Nanning China 121 D6
Nantes France 62 D4
Napier NZ 134 G4
Naples Italy 73 F6
Narsarsuaq Greenland
51 E8
Nashville USA 29 E3
Nasik India 117 E5
Nassau Bahamas 43 E2
Nasser, Lake Egypt 90 D4
Natal Brazil 46 H4
Nauru (Country) 128 D4
Navarin, Cape Rus. Fed.
113 H2
Navoi Uzbekistan 111 E3
Naxos (I.) Greece 79 F6
N'djamena Chad 94 D4
Ndola Zambia 97 C6
Nebit Dag Turkmenistan
110 C3
Nebraska (State) USA
33 F4
Negro (R.) Brazil 46 C4

Acknowledgements

Dorling Kindersley would like to thank:
Hilary Bird, Helen Chamberlain, Tricia Grogan, and Michael Williams for the index; Kate Eager and Tony Chung for design assistance; Sasha Heseltine and Caroline Brooke for editorial assistance; Paul Donnellon for editorial research p122; James Mills-Hicks and Yak El-Droubie for cartographic assistance;

Picture credits: t=top b=bottom c=centre l=left r=right
The publisher would like to thank the following for their kind permission to reproduce the photographs:

NASA, 13 tr; Science Photo Library/David Parker 15 br.

Every effort has been made to trace the copyright holders and we apologise in advance for any unintentional omissions. We would be pleased to insert the appropriate acknowledgement in any subsequent edition of this publication.